D0486035

ATTENTION HIJACKED

Advance praise for
Attention Hijacked

"A helpful guide to understanding why our relationship
to technology is so complicated, with realistic strategies
for taking back our own time, attention, and lives."

—Dr. Christopher Willard, author of *Growing Up Mindful*

"This is an important book for our times and an
indispensable resource for parent and teens alike.
Weaving together heartfelt examples, the latest data,
and practical tips, Erica Marcus's book charts the course
to a healthier way of relating to technology. Accessible,
relevant, and wise, this is a book for our times."

—Oren Jay Sofer, author of *Say What You Mean:
A Mindful Approach to Nonviolent Communication*

ATTENTION
HIJACKED

Using Mindfulness to Reclaim Your Brain from Tech

Erica B. Marcus

ZEST BOOKS
MINNEAPOLIS

To Shiloh and Zoe, for helping me see the world anew

Scan the QR codes throughout to access audio of guided mindfulness techniques.
Or visit qrs.lernerbooks.com/attentionhijacked.

Copyright © 2022 by Erica B. Marcus
Illustrations copyright © 2022 by Lerner Publishing Group, Inc.

All rights reserved. International copyright secured. No part of this book may
be reproduced, stored in a retrieval system, or transmitted in any form or by any
means—electronic, mechanical, photocopying, recording, or otherwise—without the
prior written permission of Lerner Publishing Group, Inc., except for the inclusion of
brief quotations in an acknowledged review.

Zest Books™
An imprint of Lerner Publishing Group, Inc.
241 First Avenue North
Minneapolis, MN 55401 USA

For reading levels and more information, look up this title at www.lernerbooks.com.
Visit us at zestbooks.net.

Illustrations by Athena Currier.
Cover and interior design element: AllNikArt/Shutterstock.com.

Designed by Mary Ross.
Main body text set in Bembo Std. Typeface provided by Monotype Typography.

Library of Congress Cataloging-in-Publication Data

Names: Marcus, Erica B., author.
Title: Attention hijacked : using mindfulness to reclaim your brain from tech / by
   Erica B. Marcus.
Description: Minneapolis : Zest Books , [2022] | Includes bibliographical references
   and index. | Audience: Ages 13–18 | Audience: Grades 7–9 | Summary: "Using
   mindfulness techniques, this book teaches readers how to intentionally take charge
   of their technology use" —Provided by publisher.
Identifiers: LCCN 2021033649 (print) | LCCN 2021033650 (ebook) |
   ISBN 9781728404677 (library binding) | ISBN 9781728417196 (paperback) |
   ISBN 9781728445465 (ebook)
Subjects: LCSH: Distraction (Psychology)—Juvenile literature. | Attention—Juvenile
   literature. | Mindfulness (Psychology)—Juvenile literature. | Technology—
   Psychological aspects—Juvenile literature.
Classification: LCC BF323.D5 M329 2022 (print) | LCC BF323.D5 (ebook) |
   DDC 153.7/33—dc23

LC record available at https://lccn.loc.gov/2021033649
LC ebook record available at https://lccn.loc.gov/2021033650

Manufactured in the United States of America
1-48528-49038-11/30/2021

Contents

Introduction

A few years back, I was scrolling through my Instagram feed when I came across an image of Miranda, my childhood best friend. She was on a beautiful white-sand tropical beach, tan and radiant, contorted into an incredible yoga pose. In contrast, I was sitting in my living room, pasty white and deeply bundled against the frigid Maine temps, nearly comatose from tech use. And I noticed something. As I stared at the pic, my throat clenched slightly. My shoulders rose up just a hair. And my stomach dropped. I had a wisp of a thought: *Ugh. I wish that was me.* This was followed by a cascade of reasons that I was better than her, in a desperate attempt to make myself feel better.

What makes this moment notable, even though this yucky feeling had happened a bajillion times while looking at Insta, was a recognition of how that image impacted me. If I think about my technology consumption like a diet, what I just ate left me feeling bloated and heavy—perhaps the equivalent of eating an entire bag of Cheetos. In the past, I might have scrolled on for thirty minutes, continuing with my day and feeling some unnamed uneasiness, but not really noticing or connecting my feelings to anything in particular. This time, though, it was clear as day. This time helped me wake up and ask myself, "Is scrolling through social media healthy for me?" The answer was a resounding no.

So then I deleted all the apps and never got on social media again. Yeah, right.

What *is* true is that this was the beginning of a long process of really waking up to how my technology use was impacting me. I was able to start noticing when my face felt hot and my muscles clenched because an email triggered me *before* shooting off a fiery response. I could acknowledge the way my mind felt deadened and my body stiff after allowing Netflix to autoplay the next episode . . . for the eighth time. I recognized that if I woke up and looked at the news on my phone first thing in the morning, I was extra grouchy toward my family as I got ready to teach school that day.

On the flip side, my awareness of some of the ways tech really served me grew as well. I was able to notice that I felt empowered by calls to action posted by friends who were promoting social justice. I was grateful for the electronic calendar that reminded me of a forgotten appointment I was supposed to go to in thirty minutes. I appreciated being able to go to a new city and use social media to easily connect with friends who I hadn't seen in years. I felt giddy and joyful from watching some of my favorite stand-up comics perform in cities across the country from the comfort of my living room. And especially as we braved the COVID-19 pandemic, I deeply appreciated being able to connect with my students, family, and friends over Zoom.

Over time, gaining awareness of how my tech habits were impacting me gave me freedom and control over how I engaged with technology. It has not meant that I have stopped using it altogether. It has not meant that I have completely stopped all my unhealthy habits. Just as I still sometimes eat Cheetos, I still sometimes mindlessly scroll through Instagram. The difference is that I have gradually shifted toward a healthier tech lifestyle, and I have tools to help me notice and reflect on both how my choices make me feel and how they support me in living my values (or not).

With this book, I would like to offer perspectives, awareness activities, and practices that can help you shift toward the relationship you want with technology, rather than the one you might just fall into (or have already fallen into). *How much time on my tech is too much time? Which parts of my online life are life-sucking, and which are life-affirming? Do I find things IRL that are meaningful and joyful?* I started asking myself these questions after more than a decade of practicing the mindfulness I learned from teachers in yoga and meditation traditions. To this day, I find I have to be very careful to not get swept up into mindless technology use. Once I became more familiar with my own struggles, pitfalls, and ways of managing my tech use, I wanted to share what had worked for me, and learn about my students' experiences, in this technologically-focused age.

After five years of teaching English, in 2016 I started teaching mindfulness to students full time, working intensively at a local STEM high school. I quickly realized that I couldn't talk about mindfulness without touching on technology, as technology has become completely integrated into all parts of our lives—especially for you currently in high school and college. My students often told me that they both loved and hated technology for the endless opportunities and endless distractions it offered. Together we puzzled over how to develop healthy relationships with these tools, and out of those many years of conversation, we created the exercises and practices in this book.

Chapter 1 is about the reasons we love technology. It can facilitate connection and allow us to collaborate creatively across space, time, and culture. We can connect with affinity groups (people who connect because of a shared interest), activists, and larger social movements led and participated in by our peers. We can find entertainment, news, and up-to-date information quickly and easily. We *need* our technology to continue to learn, connect, and be a part of the world. This was especially true during the COVID-19 pandemic that engulfed us in 2020. Our screens are extremely valuable, and I am incredibly grateful for the opportunities they provide.

And—this is an *And* with a capital *A*—we also need to acknowledge some very real concerns about technology use. In chapter 2, I explore how tech companies intentionally design their products to keep you hooked as long as possible and mine your data to earn as much money as possible. As one of my students put it, even if you don't care that companies are manipulating you, it is important to know about it so you can make the choice to opt in. Then, in chapter 3, we'll explore some common myths and questions around how technology use can impact our mental and physical health. Spoiler alert: it's far more complicated than any headline would have us believe.

Even more importantly, you must pay attention to yourself to collect real-time data on how *you* are being impacted by technology. How do you do that? Chapter 4 introduces one way: mindfulness. Mindfulness is as simple as paying attention to this moment, to what's happening on the inside and outside. We often think we are already paying attention. *Don't I already* know *what I'm up to? I am me, living my life, after all.* But when we start to practice mindfulness, we notice how often we are *not* paying attention. Our minds are constantly wandering. One minute you are walking to school, and the next you are back in last night's argument with your mom, and then you rocket forward to tonight when you will confidently and gleefully explain to your mom why she's wrong. The ability of our minds to time travel, to go back and forward in time, remembering and planning, is an incredible gift. But we often don't even realize it's happening, and that flitting about takes us away from how we interact with the world in real time. Mindfulness gives us a way to pause and check in with ourselves, turning research into *me*-search.

We can then take this skill of intentionally directing our attention and shine the spotlight right on our tech habits. The good news is that our brains are designed to rewire themselves through a process called neuroplasticity. It actually changes the physical structures of our brains. Though it may require some effort, even those of us who feel addicted to our tech can change neuropathways and regain a sense of agency. Chapter 5 offers some general guidelines about how to apply mindfulness to your tech usage. It gives you a survey to more closely examine how you use technology and how it might be impacting you.

Chapter 6 invites you to think about the specifics of how *your* attention gets hijacked, along with ways you can create more balance in your life. If you are newer to owning a phone or to technology in general, this is still a great section to explore, to prepare you for challenges that may arise in the future. You get to role-play some of the scenarios without experiencing the damage that can happen.

Finally, in chapter 7, we look at living your best life. Are you happy with the ways your life is unfolding, with and without your phone? Are you getting enough playtime, physical time, downtime, and sleep time? Are you content with yourself? Do you have things you like to do and people you like to be with?

Throughout this book, you'll see big-picture journal prompts in the margins. These are great ways to gain clarity about how technology functions in your life. You can use them one at a time or collectively. So grab your journal, a pen and paper—or even a Google Doc if that's going to make it happen—and get writing. Or you might discuss the ideas with friends, teachers, or parents.

By the end of this book, you should have a much better sense of the ways you engage with technology, how it impacts you, and what to do to create healthier habits. I hope you will feel empowered, inspired, and excited to really explore your own life and build a healthy relationship with yourself and your technology.

How to Use This Book

My first word of advice: don't just believe anything I say. One of my favorite things about working with teenagers is that they don't just blindly accept things. Research it for yourself. Investigate on your own. Ask questions. At the same time, I invite you to stay humble and open to the possibility that you might learn something. Only then can you be surprised, amazed, and empowered. Only then can you create a healthy technology diet that works for you.

New Tech Users

Some of you may be newer tech users. Perhaps you have had a tablet or a school laptop for a while, and you are reading this book in preparation to get a phone. If so, welcome! And, *lucky*! You have the clear advantage of not having developed any bad habits or discovered those pitfalls that others of us have already realized. Creating healthy, useful habits from the get-go is much easier than having to go back and change habits. I hope this book can serve as a road map for you to consider the ways you can set yourself up for a healthy relationship with your new device. You might find some of the sections are more or less useful to you, so feel free to skip around as it makes sense.

Experienced Tech Users

For those who are no strangers to tech and may have developed some less-than-ideal habits, this book gives you some space and time to reflect on your tech use. For the time being, can you suspend defensiveness? Can you try to open yourself up to considering how your habits may be impacting you? This is like a giant lab experiment, and your experience with tech is what you're studying. The more open and curious you are, the more you can set up habits that work for, instead of against, you.

For All Readers

This book is not meant to tell you what you *should* do. It has no opinions or judgments about how you spend your time. The intention is to share the most accurate information possible at this moment and give you some ways to investigate your own habits, whether you are just building them or you are well practiced already. Is it possible that we will learn more and develop an even clearer understanding with time and research? I sure hope so. Our understanding of this topic is ever evolving.

Furthermore, this book and mindfulness, the approach I will be talking a lot about, are not meant to be a cure-all. Mindfulness is a way of looking at our lives that can provide clarity. If you are struggling with mental health, professionals exist who can support and guide you, and this is not meant as a substitute for therapy.

Listen, I have an obvious bias here. I believe it is really easy for us as humans to get sucked into mindless technology use, and I think that sometimes makes us feel like crap. I believe there are forces at work that make it hard to put the phone or video controller or computer screen down. And I believe that we do have control over ourselves and our choices, but only if we are paying enough attention to notice what's going on. If I thought there was nothing wrong and no problem to solve, I wouldn't have written this book. If I thought there was nothing to be done about it, I wouldn't have written this book. I hear my students say that they recognize their technology use is a problem for them. Sometimes the issues they identify line up with the concerns of the adults in their lives, but sometimes they don't. I can see for myself the way tech use is problematic for me and other adults around me. I want to be clear: This is not just a concern for young people. Though the specifics of the challenges around tech use may be generational, the modern struggle for balance and wellness affects all ages.

I am a mother of two young kiddos (ages one and four at the time of publication), which means I am grappling with how to best support them in developing their own healthy relationships with technology. For now, it is easy because I can just turn off the iPad after one episode or take away the phone after the timer dings. But at some point, I need to transfer that power to them so they can start noticing and making their own choices about the impact their tech use has on them. Of course, they will make mistakes. Of course, I will make mistakes. But I'm hoping, much as I do with my students, that we can figure it out together.

Mindfulness basically asks us to take off our judgy pants for a second and really look at our experiences, especially the ones we think we already know. When we fully pay attention, defenses down, hearts open, we can be amazed by how much more there is to learn. By hearts open, I mean we can do this work with care. We can do it because we care . . . about ourselves, about our families and friends, and about the larger community. Acknowledging that we truly do want what is best for all can help us make moves that might not feel easy. Perhaps we create a social justice post to highlight the ways we can better care for one another and this world. Perhaps we put our phones down to really show care to the people we love.

Speaking of those you love, bring someone on this journey with you! Ask your friends to read along. I'll tell you what, this journey is going to be way easier if you can do it with people you care about and who care about you. If you have group habits that affect one another, this could be the perfect opportunity to discuss some of those. Do you all tend to sit around on your phones, ignoring one another aside from sharing random funny videos? Do you have the sense that maybe there is more to having relationships with other humans, but you've forgotten what you even like to do together? Notice which phone habits make it harder to spend time together and decide what choices might help strengthen your friendships. Use this book to talk through some of those things, acknowledge what's hard, and set up some guidelines together.

Tips for Talking to Parents (and Other Adults) So They Don't Automatically Shut You Down

"You're the one with the problem, not me! *You* should be reading this book!" began no successful conversation ever.

If you really want to have a conversation with your parents, it helps to remember that they're humans. Reactive, imperfect humans who want to be treated with respect and kindness just as much as you do. Inviting them into any difficult conversation, including one about technology habits, will require you to do some pre-thinking about when, how, and why. Consider the following guidelines:

- Approach them in a moment when everyone's chill.
- Approach them at a time when there's opportunity to talk (not five seconds before you are trying to get out the door to school in the morning).
- Ask if it's a good time for *them* to talk (and if it's not, ask when might be better).
- Explain your perspective and be inviting in your language. No one wants to be blamed, ridiculed, or talked down to.
- Ask for what you want, rather than telling them what they should do.
- Be open to hearing their perspective.

I don't know your parents. I can't say how they are going to hear you. But I do think it's worth a try to have civil conversations with them, for everyone's sake.

And then there's our parents and guardians. One of the biggest complaints I hear from my students is that their parents are worse than they are. Adults are the ones whose tech use causes them to ignore their kids when they are trying to talk to them, who take calls at the dinner table, and who post inappropriate and unapproved pictures on social media. So invite them to read with you. Show them that you are willing to take a look at your habits and ask that they do the same for you. Rather than fighting over a technology issue in the moment, what might it look like to preemptively start a conversation separate from a tense exchange? At the very least, it puts you in the driver's seat and shows them that you are handling technology maturely.

Next, grab an adult near you and invite them to read the next section.

For Parents, Teachers, and Other Caring Adults

While this book is written for a teen audience, there's plenty in here for adults to tackle as well! So if you're an adult reading this, I'm not going to presume what kind of approach you've taken with the young person in your life. But I have heard from many teens that they wish adults would take more time to talk with them and less time lecturing them. This can be hard when you care so deeply for your kids and want the absolute best for them, especially in this day and age when it seems like daily headlines trumpet the negative effects of tech use. When teens were younger, we could easily put blocks, limits, and boundaries around their interactions with technology. As they get older, it is time to start supporting them in figuring out how to do those things for themselves. Like any other life experience, they are going to mess up (as are we), overuse, and engage in unhealthy habits. The question remains, how do we support them through all of this? I think the best thing families can do for teens is to have regular, open conversations about how they want to be in the world, and how they want tech to play into those values.

I don't know about you, but I find myself constantly having to work at finding the right balance. One of the things I find most valuable when talking with my students is to simply own what I find are my biggest struggles, instead of telling them what I think is best for them. I then ask, with genuine curiosity, about their experiences. It opens up space for us all to talk about what's hard (and awesome) about living with technology. This book can help facilitate that conversation by highlighting areas where you might also find difficulties. Use it to foster dialogue. Talk to the young person in your life about the parts of the book you found most relatable, worrisome, or compelling. Better yet, ask them which parts were most striking for them, and really listen fully to their answers.

You can learn a lot just by listening to kids. The world is different from the one we grew up in. I didn't have a mobile phone or social media until college and a smartphone came well after that. I had an entire childhood before modern tech became a reality. I can't fully comprehend what it would be like to grow up in a world where my relationships were mediated by technology. The closest I can come is simply listening to young people. One piece of advice that has really stuck with me came from Jeremy, a teen from Virginia, who said, "One of the biggest mistakes I see parents make is they try to relate too much. While both generations have issues, it's not the same and they don't fully understand. Parents should just acknowledge the generation gap, and be open to listening and understanding."

So, as you read this book, I encourage you to be vulnerable with the young people in your life. Model owning your struggles. Invite them to share theirs. Sit on the same side of the table and problem-solve together rather than fight. We all want less fighting. Be open to the possibility that you are in this together.

I Heart Screens

It will introduce forgetfulness. . . . They will not practice using their memory because they will put their trust in [it]. . . . You provide your students with the appearance of wisdom, not with its reality. Your invention will enable them to hear many things without being properly taught, and they will imagine that they have come to know much while for the most part they will know nothing.

Does this sound like something an adult in your life might say about tech use? A teacher? In fact, it was the philosopher Socrates who said it in 370 BCE. About *writing*! People have always been afraid of advancements in technology. Socrates was terrified that the simple act of writing was the downfall of the human mind. I don't know about you, but I sure appreciate the written word. Similarly, current experts are crying out about . . . digital technology. So, let's take a moment to remind ourselves what we *love* about tech before jumping to criticize it. After all, it is incredibly useful and important.

Ish got real in the spring of 2020 when the global COVID-19 pandemic surged around the world. Suddenly, with schools, stores, and offices shuttered, it was impossible to meet some of our basic needs without devices. We started meeting as school communities through online video platforms, ordering grocery deliveries to our homes with smartphone apps, and even working remotely. We could no longer see our friends and extended family in person, so we *had* to use our phones and computers to hang out with them. We needed to read the news to know the most up-to-date information on how to stay safe in a world of shifting recommendations. Simultaneously, a national movement to protect the lives and well-being of people of color reignited, crystallizing the importance of social media and news outlets, which allowed people to stay connected to the movement and participate, from coast to coast and beyond. Through this upheaval, we relied heavily on our technology to support all aspects of our lives.

As you read this chapter, notice which aspects of tech use are most important to you, and consider how that plays out in your life. You might even discover new ways of engaging with technology that will help you feel more whole, connected, and fulfilled.

Connections

It's the only way I can stay in contact with a lot of my friends because they are far away or go to another school and I don't get to see them as often as I want to.

—Chloe, twelfth grader

As Chloe points out, tools such as text messaging, social media, and video streaming allow us to keep relationships alive, regardless of distance. If you really connect with someone you meet at camp or a concert, they can easily become a lifelong friend through technology, even if they live far from you. When I went to summer camp, I sometimes exchanged a few letters with new friends, but those relationships quickly dwindled, regardless of how valuable they felt. During the time of social distancing, when we weren't even seeing friends who might live one street over, online contact became a critical way to invest in existing friendships. Those with more time on their hands even strengthened relationships that may have otherwise fizzled, through text chains, sharing memes, and video streaming. We may also find we can connect with people we've never actually met in person through video streaming, social media, and chat sites. I work with a team of people who live across the country, many of whom I've never sat with in the same room. I still feel a strong bond with these people as we come together over video meetings, share our stories and worries, and work on projects together. Students tell me about genuine relationships they've built with eSports teammates they've competed with but never met in person.

Furthermore, many families are scattered across the country and even the globe. When I was a kid, my grandparents lived ten hours away by car, and I saw them once or twice a year. I always wondered what our bond would have felt like if we had spent more time together than these sporadic visits. But now, though my daughter's grandparents live across the country, she regularly interacts with them in a real-time, tangible way through technology. With our elders being a particularly vulnerable part of the population during the COVID-19 crisis, technology might have been the only way you could connect with your grandparents during that time. Elsie, an eighth grader from Maine, writes, "My grandmother lives in a nursing home, and throughout COVID-19, she has been feeling especially lonely. We set her up with a phone and I send her weekly updates that her nurses help her see. She now can be a part of our lives while still keeping her safe." Technology becomes massively important when traditional ways of being together are limited.

Red Flags!

While the online world can offer us amazing opportunities to connect with like-minded people, we also need to be careful about what we share in virtual spaces. We may feel a real sense of connection online with someone we have never met in person. However, we don't have any proof of who that person is or if their story is true. You may be familiar with a phenomenon called *catfishing*, in which an individual pretends to be someone they are not. At best, this is misleading and annoying. At worst, catfishing is scary and, if the person is a predator, potentially dangerous. Countless news stories tell of teens being "groomed" by online predators who catfished them by building relationships and trust before asking for sexy photos, money, or personal details that expose teens to identity fraud and other dangers.

No matter how real a connection feels, it is incredibly important not to share personally identifying information online with folks we've never met.

Details you should never share with a stranger, no matter how close you feel to them:

- Full name
- Address
- Telephone number
- Medical information
- Parents' names
- Current location or geotags

Affinity Groups

We all crave connection with people who have similar life experiences and interests. Some people seek discussions of fan fiction, sports, or art. My students join communities around shared loves of gaming, film, travel, and more. As a member of the dinosaur Facebook generation, I am in a local mom group, a fitness group, and many groups about mindfulness and meditation. These groups allow me to discuss problems and reflections with people who can relate to me, even though we have never been in the same physical place.

Not everyone finds acceptance and community where they live, especially if their identity doesn't match the dominant culture in that place. My students have talked about being LGBTQIA+ in areas where local classmates or family might not accept them. Online, they can find other people like them who might also be looking to connect and relate through their shared experience. Through online forums, they can share their real struggles of feeling isolated or discriminated against and build a more positive relationship with their shared identity. This could also be true for folks who are politically liberal in a conservative area or conservative in a liberal area, those who don't share the same religious beliefs as others in their community, or those who have an ethnicity or skin color different from people around them. Online forums can become places to discuss things with like-minded individuals and find connection with others who feel similarly disconnected. That said, always remember to use caution when sharing personal information with strangers online.

Teen Activism and Social Movements

Thanks to technology, never before have teens had such a public platform to create social change. From the 2018 Parkland, Florida school shooting survivors who tirelessly advocate for gun control legislation to climate-change activist Greta Thunberg and beyond, young people have taken the megaphone. Online platforms give space and power to young people who may not have been heard in the past. Furthermore, social media services allow others around the world to follow and join these movements. Activists can create local chapters to broaden the call for justice, equity, and human rights and in turn build a global movement. Through social media, you can either join one of these causes or start your own.

Get Involved by Exploring These Online Activist Movements

STUDENT-LED HANDLES

@AlabedBana An eleven-year-old activist, author, and Syrian refugee who speaks out against the atrocities of war.

@marchforourlives A group formed on the heels of the Parkland school shooting, launched by survivor Emma González and others, that advocates for stricter gun laws.

@GretaThunberg A youth climate activist who has famously called on world leaders to address the climate crisis.

@iammarleydias Launched the #1000blackgirlbooks campaign to collect and distribute books focusing on Black female protagonists.

@JazzJennings_ Trans activist who promotes self-love and acceptance in the LGBTQIA+ community as well as addressing policy issues that impact the well-being of trans people.

@LittleMissFlint Teen activist Mari Copeny helps kids raise their voices against toxic water in Michigan and beyond.

Information

For better or worse, you can learn just about anything on the internet. Most of us will probably try to answer our questions by using a search engine. It can be hard to remember how incredible that is. Having an index of nearly all the world's information was not a thing as recently as my childhood—and I'm thirty-seven, for perspective. Search engines are incredibly powerful tools that open up a whole range

HASHTAGS INCLUDING STUDENT VOICES

#BlackLivesMatter This movement was started by Alicia Garza, Opal Tometi, and Patrisse Cullors to organize "local power to intervene in violence inflicted on Black communities by the state and vigilantes."

#fastfashion After leading environmental organizations started critiquing the fashion industry for excessive waste, pollution, and human rights violations, young people picked up the cause.

#MeToo A movement begun by Tarana Burke in 2006 that gained traction in 2017, bringing attention to instances of sexual abuse and misconduct.

#StopLine3 This effort is led by Indigenous people (reminiscent of the work of the Dakota Access Pipeline protests #NoDAPL fight) to end the construction of a tar sands pipeline through Minnesota.

#StopAsianHate A movement addressing the anti-Asian sentiment and violence that became particularly potent during the coronavirus pandemic.

of information we couldn't have found without them—or at least couldn't have found as easily and quickly.

While Google is definitely the most popular search engine, it's certainly not the only option. For example, DuckDuckGo doesn't collect your personal information (as Google does). Ekoru donates 60 percent of proceeds to initiatives addressing climate change.

Maybe you'd like some kind of filter on the kinds of information you pull up. Encyclopedia.com gives access to "over 200 individual encyclopedias and reference books." Also, some search engines are specifically designed for academic purposes, so the links have already been vetted as trustworthy sources of information. Google Scholar is the number one search engine for academic purposes, and it usually has sources that your teachers will respect as valid (though you still ought to be a responsible consumer). And while you probably shouldn't go citing it in your papers, crowd-sourced Wikipedia can be a great place to start researching any topic. Wikipedia articles often include sources that you can use to verify the information you read and go into more depth.

Having this relatively uncensored access to information can be really helpful. Teens haven't always gotten the most accurate information on topics such as sexual health, for example, because schools and parents can be uncomfortable or restrictive about it. Now tons of resources on sites like Scarleteen are at your fingertips. If you find the right sources, you can safely find information about subjects you may find embarrassing, uncomfortable, or unsafe to discuss in person.

Furthermore, you can use online platforms to discover and hone new hobbies. Eighth grader Amelia says, "I really enjoy doing intricate makeup looks. I developed my skills and now get most of my inspiration from other people on social media. I have a lot of fun and have improved a lot over the past year." For the record, I've seen her work. It's really cool.

Lulu, a seventh grader, watches online videos to help hone her athletic skills. She told me, "I use YouTube to learn tricks for

> # Journal Prompt
>
> Why do *you* love your technology?
> What are all the reasons and ways you use it?

all sports. I took at least six to ten months to actually land my first kickflip on a skateboard, and I had no lessons, no tips, but YouTube was almost like my coach. I would get frustrated when I couldn't land one, so I would go looking for different tips until one finally worked for me."

Not only can you get information on topics that hit close to home, like your own health and hobbies, but you can learn about foreign countries and cultures. One of my high school students told me she was able to use technology to organize a study abroad experience with students from all over the world. If you can't actually travel, you can take a virtual tour of the streets of any city in the world. You can follow people on social media who live four time zones away and learn about their culture and daily lives. You can learn new languages through apps and online programs. Technology makes the global stage much smaller and creates huge potential to build cross-cultural understanding.

Finally, news sources are streaming information 24-7. While there is undoubtedly a dark side to this if we find ourselves glued to streaming news or misled by fake news, we can also quickly learn about important events. We can access in-depth reporting and global perspectives on what's happening in our country. For example, the BBC, a news organization in the United Kingdom, can offer a different lens on events in the United States than a local news source. Having this outside perspective helps us broaden our understanding and gain a more complete picture of what is happening around us.

I Heart Screens 25

Who Says?: How to Be Internet Wise

It can be really hard to sift through what is fake and real on the internet these days. Anyone can post and have their words recirculated, so we must be careful. The *Oxford English Dictionary* even made "post-truth" the Word of the Year in 2016, illustrating how some "news" sources center less on objective fact and more on firing up their readership.

I once made the mistake in class of quoting a "study" that claimed humans have "less of an attention span than a goldfish." My students, brilliant as they are, were immediately skeptical and called me out. *How do you measure the attention span of a goldfish? Of a human? The decline of the attention span? That sounds like pseudoscience meant to promote pop psychology!*

Okay then. It was clear I needed to go back and dig deeper. I had found that quote in *Time* magazine, a fairly reputable source, but I wasn't sure where the reporter had found that information. I went back to try to get to the bottom of it, and found my searches simply led me in circles, each article quoting another article quoting this fun fact. But is it true? At the end of the day, I couldn't find the evidence. This showed me that if I really wanted to find truth on the internet, it could be a more intensive process than I had bargained for.

I hope you use a similar skeptical lens when you hear "facts" and "statistics." Even our best sources misstep. Here are some general guidelines that can help you evaluate sources:

- Can you find multiple sources that confirm the information?
- Where did the information start? Images and stories get shared at the speed of light, but figuring out their origin can help you assess accuracy.

- Are the people speaking experts on the subject? Why should we believe them?
- Does this person have a clear bias that might skew the truth?
- What are the fonts on the page? All caps and silly fonts are immediate red flags.
- URLs that end in .edu, .org, and .gov tend to be more reliable than .com and .net.

So go forth and learn from sources on the internet, but do so with caution and attention!

Education

Not too long ago, knowledge was restricted to the elite. If you went to a well-funded school, you had access to more information through academia. If you had a set of expensive, up-to-date *Encyclopedia Britannica*, you were able to learn about ideas, places, and people that were not in your immediate experience. These days, everyone can access knowledge in the public domain. You can learn about nearly anything through free online courses. Websites such as Khan Academy or Duolingo can teach you new skills and languages, and you can look up a YouTube video for nearly any math problem you may be struggling through. Knowledge has become much more accessible to all.

Of course, sussing out what is true and real from what is invented requires a great amount of thought and attention. We must use a critical eye to look at everything we see, because anyone can present their opinion as fact. But we have the opportunity to develop that critical-thinking capacity and use it to learn about anything we want, all from the safety of our own couch.

And then there's formalized education. While going to school with other students in a building works for many, technology has made alternative schooling methods possible. Those who want a more flexible program have turned to online school, where the pacing is self-led and responsive to student time constraints. This kind of learning can be appealing to many students, from those who are semiprofessional athletes, to those who don't find success in brick-and-mortar school learning, to those who may just want to pick up an extra class not offered in their local school. A friend of mine is a science teacher at the Virtual Learning Academy Charter School in New Hampshire. The school caters to students like Emily, a competitive dancer who finds relief in the adaptable structure that allows her to work around her intensive dance schedule.

Online classes are available both at the grade school and collegiate level. I took a number of college-level courses entirely online, and I appreciated being able to do assignments at my own pace and learn from the comfort of my home.

Additionally, the COVID-19 pandemic has shown us that staying safe can require periods of time when we are physically apart. In this context, we need an alternative means for continuing our education. Learning platforms such as Google Classroom, Zoom, Padlet, Flipgrid, and Nearpod provided a way for learning to continue. The sudden shutdown of schools required teachers and students to immediately develop a whole new skill set around learning online. This was incredibly difficult for everyone involved (am I right?), but without technology, our formal education would have come to a standstill. If, in the future, hazards again keep us apart, we will be more prepared for an alternative learning structure. Furthermore, as we move away from lockdown, we may notice the ways that online learning did work better than in-person. (For example, it can be super helpful to rewatch a video of your teacher explaining something as many times as you want.) If we pay attention, we can undoubtedly figure out better ways to use technology to enhance learning.

Online Courses

Interested in doing some learning? Check out the following options to take courses and receive an education online. Keep in mind that these are just a few of the many possibilities available.

Coursera Free courses from universities and top companies, including certificate and degree programs.

Duolingo Fun, free app- and web-based program that gamifies language learning.

edX Free courses with titles including "Science & Cooking: From Haute Cuisine to Soft Matter Science" and "The Einstein Revolution," available to anyone. Top schools including Harvard University; University of California, Berkeley; and MIT have offerings here.

Open Culture More than fifteen hundred free online courses from a whole host of top universities.

Skillshare Creative subscription-based classes in illustration, photography, graphic design, and more.

Creativity

I had the opportunity to chat with two brothers, Evan and Jeremy, who are both deep into creative pursuits online. Evan is a cinephile (full transparency: I had to look up this word. It's a person who is really into movies) and filmmaker. For creative inspiration, he uses Letterboxd and subreddits to delve deep into the art of filmmaking with like-minded individuals. He watches a ton of content, from serious films to TikTok videos. He then turns around and creates his own work, shooting with a camera or simply his iPhone. Some of Evan's works are for a school film class, while others are comedies and sketches he posts on TikTok. Technology has aided his work from start to finish: it allows him to find inspiration, learn about the process of filming, connect with a larger community of film appreciators and makers, create his own work, and share it.

Evan's brother, Jeremy, goes through a similar process with music creation. He listens to a ton of music online and then uses specialized software to produce his own. He uses music annotation software to write his pieces, other tools to record and layer different instrument tracks, and adds recordings created by other artists. Then he shares the final product on streaming sites to build an audience. These examples demonstrate how technology and online sources can provide creative fuel. So too can art and music courses, access to highly regarded artists and performers, and virtual museums. Once inspiration has struck, many platforms can help you to produce, share, and collaborate on work.

To this last point, collaboration has been proven to lead to more creative results. Technology can remove the barriers of time and space. We can watch videos of performers who have layered their work over that of others to produce a collab despite physical distance or time zones. TikTok is full of these duets, where we watch performers dance, sing, or respond to the content of another. In a more formal setting, technology can bring new voices to workplaces that may have otherwise been inaccessible because of geography or disabilities. Quite a few studies have found that diverse teams are more innovative than those made up of folks with similar identities. Working virtually can allow for a greater diversity of perspectives to come together from across the country and globe, without the necessity of physically gathering.

Like time and distance, cost can also become less of a barrier online. Colleges and other educational sites are offering more and more free or low-cost courses to support talent development. For example, open online education provider edX has more than twenty-five hundred free courses, many of which specifically focus on art and music. Furthermore, those who work in creative fields often study experts in their area to spark their own creativity. Listening to and learning from those we admire can help us hone our own talents. Thanks to the internet, artists are more available than ever, both in terms of sharing their craft and offering a behind-the-scenes glimpse into their lives. Whereas brick-and-mortar art museums may feel inaccessible because of distance or cost, we can readily view art through their online platforms. And streaming platforms such as Spotify, SoundCloud, and Bandcamp offer a whole range of musical genres and artists, at a lower price point than going to in-person shows.

In addition to discovering inspiration, there's no shortage of digital tools for creation. Artists often draw and manipulate images online. Computer-aided design (CAD) software allows us to draw and visualize projects that we can actually create on 3D printers. Photographers take, edit, and print photos through numerous apps. Musicians write, record, and mix musical numbers. We can create beautiful infographics, slideshows, and graphic representations. While this all used to require tons of expensive equipment, newer free and low-cost tech has made it easier for the everyday person to create and finish their own work themselves.

And finally, you can easily share your work on digital platforms. YouTube hosts films and music. Sites such as Teen Ink publish poetry, short stories, and essays. You can upload your music to SoundCloud. Technology is supporting the creative process from top to bottom, allowing for impressive, collaborative innovation.

Organization

It can be hard to stay on top of all your assignments, commitments, and family obligations. Shared digital calendars that you can access through your phone or laptop are incredibly helpful in keeping everything organized and meeting deadlines. Many teachers put everything on an online classroom, so you may not even need a paper planner. You can set reminders on your phone to help keep it all straight. You can also create to-do lists on your phone, which can sync to your tablet or computer, rather than writing on paper sticky notes that melt in the washer when you forget to take them out of your pocket.

Assignments will never physically disappear if you are working on them in the cloud. (Okay, never say never. Strange tech glitches happen on occasion.) Filing assignments in virtual folders is much easier than using the paper folders we all used to carry around and sort through. Using tech also means you won't spill peanut butter on your assignments while completing them, and your teachers also won't spill peanut butter on your assignments when grading them. Additionally, an internet connection lets you submit work to your teacher anytime with just the click of a button.

Setting reminders and timers, using calendars and to-do lists, and having a centralized place where assignments can't get lost are key to helping us stay organized.

Organizational Tips

File system: File assignments into folders on your personal drive. Online, this might mean you have an electronic folder for each class. Maybe you will break the folders down into different topics within a class or a unit of study, so that you can easily find the materials you need to study for a test.

Labels: Label your documents clearly and specifically, so you know what's in there. Calling a file "Erica Marcus Book" is not as useful as naming it "Attention Hijacked Book Notes," and keeping it in my "Books" folder.

Tabs, tabs, tabs: Sometimes as I work at my computer, I find that I have twenty or thirty tabs open in the same browser window. (Sound familiar?) The tabs get so small I can't read the titles, and I have to click through to find what I need. To fix that, I started creating windows of tabs that are all in the same theme. One window is dedicated to articles and resources I find personally interesting that I might like to come back to. One is currently dedicated to this book and includes open notes and draft tabs. Another holds my work email and a few relevant and time-sensitive documents pulled up. When I am working in one window, I minimize the other windows so I can't see them. Also, I periodically close everything down, mostly to prove to myself that if I really need it, I can find it again. Everything else was probably just clutter.

Schedule it: An electronic calendar is an amazing tool. You can share calendars with your parents so they know when and where your soccer game is, and you can remember their upcoming anniversary weekend away. During the pandemic, many teachers used online classroom suites that automatically generate assignment deadlines, which you can customize if you need to chunk out assignments (read chapter 1 by Tues, chapters 2 and 3 for Wed, and so on). Using different colors for different classes, sports practices and games, and friend hangouts can be helpful, so you can easily see what's coming. I find it really useful to make time each week to sit down with my calendar and update the week ahead.

Study space: As much as possible, make sure the physical space where you set up your computer is clear of clutter and distractions. Having your own desk is ideal, if it's possible. The more pleasant and clean your workspace is, the easier it will be to settle in and focus. And the number one distraction, which should be not just be flipped over but instead placed out of sight is . . . your phone! Put it in another room during study time, or at least zip it into your backpack.

These suggestions are inspired by Samantha Moss's book *Where's My Stuff? The Ultimate Teen Organizing Guide.*

Entertainment

Entertainment (*noun*): a form of activity that holds the attention and interest or gives pleasure and delight. So says Wikipedia (and yes, I'm citing Wikipedia, because I like their definition, not necessarily because it has authority). This is a pretty broad category, but for our purposes, we are talking about entertainment as something we do just for funsies. And there is a bottomless pit of entertaining content online. Through our technology, we can find hilarious stand-up comedy routines, silly cat videos and memes, beautiful nature images, exquisite video games, articles about interesting people, threads about the best way to open a can, and much more. It can be worthwhile to indulge in our own happiness just for the sake of bringing ourselves joy. I like to watch a series of ridiculous videos in which dogs are dressed in various costumes, looking unamused. I like doing online crossword puzzles because I find it fun to challenge my mind. I enjoy the rapid-fire cooking videos where they create a cake in two minutes or less. Laughter and amusement can be helpful for our mental wellness.

Furthermore, many of us bond over online content. It can offer a point of connection to everyone else who has seen, played, or read the thing you were checking out. Many of my students connect over shared experiences gaming, watching the same YouTube videos, and sharing ridiculous memes. Some of them watch and attempt to put their own spin on viral TikTok videos together. The world can feel like a heavy place, and light, fun experiences can help lift our spirits.

As we start to explore some of the concerns of tech use, let us not forget the ways that technology serves us. We can use it to connect and collaborate with others, access infinite amounts of information and ideas of the world, pursue artistry and creativity, organize and join social movements to create change, organize our ideas and lives, and find humor and lightness. We can use these positives to keep perspective and help guide the ways we want to engage with technology.

CHAPTER 2

How Tech Companies Hijack Our Attention

You're deeply engrossed in a video game, a show series, or a social media platform, and all of a sudden you look up, bleary eyed, and it's two a.m. You immediately wonder, *Wait, what? How the heck did that happen?* Well, it certainly didn't happen by accident. A ton of money and expertise gets dumped into figuring out how to keep you on your screen a little longer, a little later, a little less aware-r of what's happening away from that screen. We like to think we are always in control of our choices, but we are being manipulated in a deep way. Like, science-fiction-unnerving levels of deep psychological manipulation.

Experts on the other side of our screens are doing everything in their power to manipulate us. What I mean is that there are people who have spent a lot of energy considering what colors make you most likely to click, what features make you most likely to keep watching, what content is most likely to keep you scrolling, and what graphics are most likely to keep you entertained. As technology engineer Aza Raskin put it, "It's as if they're taking behavioral cocaine and just sprinkling it all over your interface and that's the thing that keeps you coming back and back and back. . . . There are generally, like, literally a thousand engineers that have worked on this thing to try and make it maximally addicting." Tech creators are constantly running experiments on us to see which way of capturing and maintaining our attention is most effective and then pivoting around that. Don't get me wrong, it's not like there's a person with a giant mug full of coffee sitting in a room monitoring you 24-7. But there *is* a room full of computers that are "watching" you and making choices, sometimes independent of human interference. And these computers are so sophisticated that they constantly monitor and adapt to your choices and behaviors to make you act the way they want you to act. And you usually do what they want you to do. Because they know you. They know your habits, patterns, behaviors, and every choice you've ever made in front of the screen.

Who runs these experiments and designs computer algorithms that monitor and change your behavior? It's actually teams of people who vary by project. Mathematicians and statisticians work out the perfect variable reward strategy (see page 42 for more on this "slot machine effect") to maximize your time-on-device. User experience designers consider how to make apps and programs as user-friendly as possible so that you don't have any frustrating hiccups that might cause you to exit. Neuroscientists, psychologists, and social scientists also contribute to technology. These experts understand the patterns of mind that dictate human behavior. They use this understanding to recommend design features that grab your attention and produce just the right hormone release to keep you coming back for more. Software engineers, coders, and programmers, alongside sound designers, technical artists, and creative directors, are the ones who know how to put these ideas into practice, of course, and bring them to life. Just a quick review of Instagram's job postings reveals titles such as "Culture & Community Marketing Manager," "Consumer Product Marketing Lead," "Technical Program Manager," "Data Science Manager," and "Instagram Shopping Demand," to name just a few. There are even entire companies with the sole job of helping other tech companies make their programs more addictive. One such company representative writes, "The dopamine API is a tool that allows any app to become addictive. The premise is really straightforward . . . people don't just love that burst of dopamine they get from a notification; it changes the wiring of the brain."

Yes, you read that right. It changes the wiring of your brain. And that rewiring makes you more likely to click and never leave. So many tiny decisions that go into this are being made at every moment, more than you or I could even know or imagine without working in these fields. But big tech companies are using some pretty blatant strategies that compel us to react—and those strategies are what we can begin to look out for.

Brain Break

Brain scientists know what kinds of experiences lead to our bodies releasing different neurotransmitters and hormones. These chemicals make us feel a certain way, which can impact how we behave. So which neurotransmitters and hormones are companies paying attention to? Let's take a quick look inside your brain to find out.

Adrenaline The adrenal glands produce this hormone in response to a stressor, which triggers that excited feeling that makes your heart pound, your body tingle, and your palms sweat. Adrenaline is released when you are playing a high-intensity video game, making it feel like you are in the action. This can create the experience of positive stress, also known as *eustress*, or over longer periods of time, distress, when the body dysregulates in response to too much adrenaline in the system.

Cortisol Also known as hydrocortisone, this hormone regulates many body processes. We get a spike of it in the morning to help us wake up, and levels fall throughout the day. We also get a hit when we encounter a stressor, which works in tandem with adrenaline to create that highly energized state that allows us to act quickly in a moment of danger (real or perceived).

Dopamine This neurotransmitter released in the brain is associated with many things, but most relevant to this conversation, it is the pleasure-producing reward chemical in our brains that makes us feel good when we are rewarded with food, money, comments on a post, or a dancing emoji text.

Oxytocin The hypothalamus in your brain produces this "social" hormone that increases feelings of connection between people. People often refer to it as the "cuddle" hormone. Your brain releases oxytocin when you give someone a hug but also when someone likes your Instagram pic.

Why do these strategies make us react? Well, they make us feel something. They toy with our very human condition, in which we have these incredibly complex and industrious nervous systems that are built to protect us and help us thrive. Our nervous system is taking in information even before our conscious mind does. And this system is trained to protect us from threats and to seek connection. That jolt that floods your body when you see you have a ton of likes on a recent photo? That nagging itchy feeling to open Snapchat when you see you have seven new notifications? Those are all due to little shifts in your neurochemistry prompting you to act. And tech companies know that. They use it against you.

Let's look at some specific ways tech companies capture your attention and keep you engaged as long as possible.

The Notification

The notification is a design feature intentionally created to cause that itch, that anxiety, that *need* to check an app. Did you ever realize that even the color red circling the numbers in the corner of our app icon was purposefully manipulative? Red is a color we associate with urgency, and it jacks up our heart rate and creates a need to act. And then there are all those dings, tweets, and buzzes alerting us that *something* has happened! The most unnerving part is the unknown aspect. My students often talk about how something can seem so important, and can *feel* so important, that they have to check it out. *I need to see whatever it is that you just sent me. What if it's important?* Having notifications turned on ensures that even if we are just trying to check the time, even if nothing buzzed, we can easily get pulled in to look more closely at who commented on our feed and what they said.

Some of my students even spoke about "phantom" notifications. This habit of checking had become so strong that they felt like they had to look, even when they knew there was nothing to see. They reported feeling anxious when they weren't allowed to have their phones out during class. They really felt like they needed to keep checking to keep their anxiety about that possible "what if?" at bay. That's powerful stuff.

Here's what one student noted:

> There are many different things I could say about the negative effects tech has had on my life. Lately, I've been experiencing, like, literal auditory hallucinations. Like, [it is] constantly in my head that [my phone is] always going off. It's always drawing my eyes back to it. It doesn't matter what I'm doing, if I'm listening to music or I'm sucked into doing art with my friends, I'll always be pulled back into it. I'll have the notifications totally muted and I'll start to hear it and I'll go totally crazy at that point because I know it's not making sounds but I'm still hearing it. . . . It's really easy to get sucked into, *Oh, there's a notification* or *Oh, I wonder if anyone posted anything funny today.* And then twenty minutes have gone by, and everyone [in my class] has been drawing for twenty minutes and I've barely started.
>
> **—Ashton, twelfth grade**

Does that feel familiar? Notifications are powerful cues to get us checking and rechecking our phones throughout the day to make sure we aren't missing anything. It may not benefit you to walk around all day in a partially distracted state, but it does benefit someone on the other end of an app. See if you can start noticing how it feels when you see and hear your alerts. Can you pause, even a moment, before reacting, just to explore how it feels in your body? What's your heart rate doing? Your breath? Is your body tingly or itching? Is it in a specific area or all over?

The Slot Machine Effect

It all started with American psychologist B. F. Skinner's research with rats in 1948. He looked at rats that were given food pellets every time they pressed a lever and compared them with rats that pressed the lever and received pellets at random times in random amounts. The rats in the variable reward group (sometimes a small treat, sometimes a big one, sometimes nothing) pressed that lever more obsessively than the regularly rewarded group in desperate hope that a treat would pop out. You can imagine that poor little rat in there going, "Commmmeee ooonn! Show me the *big one!*" with its little paw going *Click! Click! clickclickclickclickclickclickCLICKCLICK!*, just waiting for the reward. This is known as the "variable rewards schedule," or "slot machine effect," because slot machine companies have made tremendous amounts of money by applying this idea to their machines. Tech companies ingeniously picked up on this idea and have used it to keep us on their platforms, sites, and games.

Any game that relies on some sort of seeking and conquest plays right into this idea. Love it or hate it, one of the most compelling video games in recent history is *Fortnite*. As one tech consultant wrote, "The main rewards *Fortnite* offers is the uncertainty around each session: you have no idea who your opponents will be, how well they play, what terrain you'll end up in, or what loot you might find once you get there. The search for variable rewards also comes in the form of ways to personalize your avatar." All of these unknowns about when and how you will be rewarded create in your body a desire to continue. If you're into gaming, think about a time when you were cut off from it. What did it feel like in your body when you suddenly couldn't keep playing and satisfy that deep need for reward? It can actually be physically uncomfortable, no? These feelings in our bodies are what make us keep playing and also what can make us explode when we are asked to stop.

Social media platforms are no different. Take Instagram. Usually, your feedback from the app, in the form of hearts and

comments, doesn't load the second you sign in. Just like the spinning of the slot machine, there's an anticipation or buildup as you wait for that reward. This makes the rush of receiving that feedback even greater when it finally comes. Each time you sign in, you don't know what kind of reward you are going to get. Twenty new likes? Three new comments on how good you look? The fact that there are different feedback rewards each time makes it even more compelling to us. We may not even consciously be having these thoughts, but they are playing out in the background all the time.

Can you slow down enough to really notice how this effect is playing out in your own body? As you open Snapchat, can you physically feel that rush? Or as you are moving through your favorite video game, and your dad calls from the other room to turn it off for dinner, what happens internally? Start taking note of the ways that games and apps make you feel as you interact with them.

The Autoplay, the Endless Stream, and the Never-Ending Game

Once you've watched that YouTube video a friend recommended, you're done, right? *Oh, but two more recommended videos just popped up and do I want to watch . . . ? Oh, it's playing. Whatever. I'll check it out.* This feature, known as *autoplay*, is found on all video platforms because once one discovered it, the rest understood the power of continuous loading. The autoplay feature doesn't give you enough time to make a decision. Momentum kicks in, and it's much easier to keep doing the thing you are already doing than to stop doing it. You end up three hours later in a puddle of drool, wondering how you got so deep down the rabbit hole and if you even have the energy for algebra. (The answer is no.)

But autoplay is not just feeding you similar content. It is intentionally recommending videos with wilder and more stimulating content precisely engineered to keep you glued to the screen. The artificial intelligence governing what gets loaded next has learned that people tend to keep watching if something creates a strong emotional reaction or confusion in your mind. Think about it: Anger is not boring. Anger makes you want to act. Confusion makes you want to resolve the problem. One of the most famous examples of this is the flat-Earth conspiracy theory perpetuated on YouTube. The YouTube computer algorithm saw that people who watched flat-Earth content were more likely to keep watching. (Because it created confusion for them, they had to resolve the discomfort of confusion. So they kept watching.) YouTube started recommending these videos more, and this theory actually gained traction and a huge following. All because YouTube wants to keep us glued to the screen for as long as possible.

Close cousin of the autoplay feature is the endless stream. One thing about social media platforms such as Instagram, Snapchat, and TikTok is that there is no ending. You can't get to the bottom. There's no place to stop. That infinite nature of the platform means you could be on forever. So, you are. This effect is so powerful that a lawmaker from Missouri, Senator Josh Hawley, introduced a bill in

2019 to combat it. The goal of the Social Media Addiction Reduction Technology (SMART) Act is to try to stop companies from providing limitless content, and instead implement time limits that users can set to protect themselves from temptation. Companies know the urge to keep watching is too strong for our mere mortal minds, and thus they have designed their platforms to keep us on. As of the time of publication, Congress has yet to act on this bill.

Many games also provide endless content. They simply never end. You could, if you had it in you, play forever. *Minecraft* is an example of a sandbox game in which you can roam free and never reach a finish line, because there isn't one. Or you can play games like *Grand Theft Auto V*, where you can complete mini missions throughout and roam freely. It can be hard to self-select an ending point in these games, because there isn't a natural one built in.

What can we mere mortals do? Start by noticing how long you are on different sites, apps, or games. How do you feel after scrolling or playing for half an hour? An hour? Two hours? Do you feel vibrant, alive, and ready to tackle problems or enjoy moments in your real life? Or do you feel spacey, sluggish, and unmotivated? This is all information that can be helpful to pay attention to. *How does getting sucked down these rabbit holes leave me feeling?*

Streaks and Punishments

Video games and social media platforms alike use a simple tool known as streaks and punishments that either reward you for getting on regularly or punish you for neglecting your poor little game or platform. Let's talk rewards. For daily logins, a game series called *Summoners War* gives you a "random prize" (ohhh . . . variable rewards at play here much?), a bunch of crystals for completing daily missions, and XP (experience points). On the flip side, you may be punished for not logging in. In the game *FarmVille*, for instance, you might plant crops that take four hours to grow. In that case, you must log back in four hours later to harvest your crops. If you don't, your plants die (unless you buy "Unwither" tools). So, the game gets either your attention or your money. These mechanisms create a need in you to come back. If you are playing these kinds of games, think about how it feels to miss out on rewards that are so easily obtained. Or how it feels to be punished because you forgot to log in at the required interval. It probably feels . . . bad.

Social media platforms do this too! Think about disappearing content like Instagram Stories or Snapchat. If you don't get on there in time to see what's there, it's gone. To stay up-to-date, you must log in regularly, or you miss out. This works in consort with the notifications. Can you imagine if someone tagged you in an Instagram Story and you got the notification, but you didn't get on the app to see exactly what content was blowing up your phone? Imagine knowing everyone else may have seen the content, but you have no idea what it was. It would likely give you a bad case of the heebie-jeebies. You're trapped.

And there's nothing like the gain or loss of a Snapstreak to keep you coming back for more. As you likely know, the longer you communicate daily back and forth with a friend on Snapchat, the longer your streak gets. That streak is represented by an increasing number count with emoji rewards to celebrate longer streaks. Some think it represents commitment to friendship, serves as a way of building friendship, and provides physical evidence of a friendship. You start to feel like you couldn't possibly put your phone down for one day or you'd risk jeopardizing that friendship.

Even teens who totally see what's going on still find it compelling and don't want to end a Snapstreak. Maybe you can relate to Chloe, a high school senior, who says, "I don't really like it. . . . Streaks I think are very dumb, but I end up snapping up back and forth with my best friend. . . . Our streak is over a year long at this point and I sort of like watching that little number go up. I don't know why. It's really stupid."

But even when we can see what's happening, and we think it's dumb, it can be hard to disentangle ourselves from the feeling of obligation. Tech designers create that feeling on purpose.

Social Drive

We need friends. All of us have an innate drive to build connections and social status. Much like chimpanzees, lions, or the most extreme example, ants, we are a communal species and rely on one another to get by. In our childhood years, our drive to connect focuses on our parents and family, but when we get into our teen years, that drive shifts. And you know who it shifts to without me even saying, right? Friends your own age. Consider our ancient ancestors, who needed to support one another in taking care of their basic needs. Surviving alone back then was nearly impossible. Our ancient ancestors preparing to leave their families 100 percent needed friends to survive. And for modern people, making connections, especially during your teen years, still actually feels like life or death. If you had lived in these early communities, it would have been.

Now we "survive" through technology, which offers endless opportunity to feel connected and build relationships with peers. Because of your age, your body reacts especially strongly to online cues that you are "in" or "out," connected or disconnected. When you have a sense of not being plugged in, your stress hormone levels shoot much higher than those of adults who already have firm networks established. Parents sometimes have a hard time understanding why their kids are so invested in social media or video games, because they physically don't get the same intense dopamine and oxytocin hits that y'all are getting from engaging when you do connect.

All social networking platforms are built around this need for connection. They turbocharge our desire with something as simple as a "like" feature or a comments section. This taps into our fiercely strong, innate need for approval and acceptance and lures us to engage more to receive the validation we crave.

Just as earlier humans once scanned the physical environment looking for opportunities to connect and build clans, we scan the virtual landscape looking for these same windows. We also scan for evidence that we don't belong. Think about how it feels when we don't get as many likes as we think we should, or the comments aren't glowing, or friends are posting about hanging out and you weren't invited. Likes, tags, and streaks can indicate approval and belonging. Catching a disappearing story can make you feel like part of the group, while missing one can make you feel left out.

These interactions are like those in the real world, but amped up, and happening constantly. You used to be able to go home and leave social jockeying at school, but now it's happening online and there are no times that you can be away from it. If you don't sign in, there's no telling what you might miss, and that is woven into the fabric of your real-time life as well.

And in some ways, online feels safer than real life because you can curate and edit the image of yourself you want to portray rather than the messy reality of being human, which often spills out with no filter. However, seeking approval through these lenses can be complex. Even though we know our online selves are not full and whole and real, we still compare our real-life selves to the online versions of others.

Online multiplayer games are another platform where you can hang out with real-life friends or make online ones. Such games have a lot of positive attributes. Players work together to solve problems, which can create a deep sense of belonging. The intensity of the experience and collaboration cements camaraderie and connection. Players go on missions together and build a relationship of trust and understanding in order to win.

However, these games also have negative attributes. The kind of social connection they provide can be addictive. Players ignore their real lives in favor of playing the game, which can lead to mental and physical health concerns. Massively multiplayer online role-playing games (MMORPGs) such as the World of Warcraft series are thought to be some of the most addictively designed games because of that social component.

What Do Tech Companies Get Out of It?

So why are tech companies designing their offerings to hijack your attention?

It's complicated.

While I am making a case about the manipulative tendencies of large tech companies, I want to also acknowledge the complexity of this world. An indie game movement has seen the creation of many games that are not primarily profit driven. And some people involved in these processes are genuinely interested in creating cool experiences for fellow humans. Many video game projects boast incredible artistry and ingenuity. They are beautifully crafted and sophisticated, with complex story lines and game play. They provide incredible opportunities to live in alternative and beautifully imaginative worlds. They are compelling because they are done so well, not necessarily because of master manipulators out to earn a buck.

Furthermore, some of the manipulative tools we've discussed are used to help people develop healthy habits and educational experiences. I use a meditation app that sends a notification to practice every day. It reports back to me my streaks and total time engaged, which are both motivating tools. I have used fitness apps that do the same thing. Duolingo, a free-to-use language learning app often assigned as homework in the school where I work, also employs streaks. Each day you sign in and play enough to meet your XP goal, you get another number next to a flame. So these tools do support us signing on again and again, but to help us learn or practice a skill that could truly be good for us. (Look out, though, because Duolingo does advertise to you within their free program.)

Even some of the tech behemoths show intentions of wanting to do good. For a long time, Google's motto was, "Don't be evil," and they meant it to encourage their employees to design in an ethical way. But those motives get muddy when companies have a simple bottom line of, *Get as many of the monies as you can.*

How do platforms make money if they are free?

They are selling you.

I'm not being dramatic here. This is for real. We are in the habit of thinking about ourselves as the consumers. We are the ones buying products, after all. We purchase the shoes, the shirts, the makeup, the phones. However, many tech companies don't actually have anything to sell us, or at least not anything up front. They let us use their search engines, social media platforms, video streaming sites, games, and online communities for free. In exchange, they get two things.

One: they get our attention.

Many companies then sell this attention to other companies that are buying and selling access to our eyes, ears, hearts, and ultimately, wallets. This exchange is known as the attention economy. At its surface, this doesn't seem that revolutionary. After all, haven't billboards, magazines, and newspapers been in the business of selling our attention through ads for a long time now? Tech companies are just doing the same thing online, right? Not exactly. As we said earlier, tech companies use the brain power of top psychologists, behavior specialists, and neuroscientists, combined with the amazing data-crunching capacity of artificial intelligence, to figure out exactly what to show you, when to show it, and how, so as to best manipulate you. How do they do this? That leads us to the second thing platforms get from us.

Two: they get our data.

Not only do tech companies have our attention moment to moment, but they get to track where our attention goes over time.

Journal Prompt

How does knowing that companies are intentionally hijacking your attention impact how you would like to use technology?

They can create a virtual profile of our age, gender, location, political leanings, relationship status, travel habits, favorite roast of coffee, and a lot of other things. Computers do this work for big tech companies by recording every search, post, click, hover, like, comment, purchase, skim, skip, amount of time on site, and more. They can then turn around and use that data to offer targeted ads to you.

This gets us back to why companies would want to keep us on platforms as long as possible. The longer they have our attention, the more opportunities they have to sell us things, whether that be through loot boxes in a video game or advertisements in our social media feed. The more data they are able to collect on us, the more targeted ads they can create for us in the future. Because they have so much data, they can target ads in a way that is creepily purposeful. Like, where to put the ad, how many times to push it out, what time of day to let it drop, which model to include in the ad, and so on.

Perhaps you think, *Hey, I really like that these companies understand me so completely that their advertising is all stuff I actually want. Then I can just get the stuff I want and need instead of seeing a bunch of random ads about things that obviously have nothing to do with me!* On its surface, there does appear to be some benefit to having your advertising stream catered to you. I know that as Instagram has gotten better at figuring me out, I find myself buying more stuff from there (especially now that there are payment options simply built in so I don't have to go find my wallet and credit card). And some of the stuff I am glad to have. But do I need that stuff? Would I have bought it without it being in my face? Probably not. A machine far more sophisticated than my measly human brain manipulated me into buying these things at a two-a.m. moment of weakness.

But, you say, *you know what, it doesn't matter because I don't even have my own income stream or credit card yet.* That's okay. Tech companies know that: (a) your parents have one or two of these things; and (b) eventually you will too. These companies are in it for the long haul. They are learning who you are as you grow up in front of them. They watch your interests, your attitudes, and your relationships change. They watch your screen habits change. They know you now, they know you as you grow, and they know human behavior. In some ways, this is even creepier than targeting ads to you. Because they won't just have data on you as an adult. They will have data on you, and all your peers, from your entire lifetime. And they will undoubtedly be a part of creating who you become—not for your benefit, but for their profit.

Take the ubiquitous Google search. This is not just a neutral repository of all the world's information. What shows up in your search, and as advertisements embedded within the websites you visit, are catered to who Google thinks you are based on your past behavior. And if you are a full-on Google user, meaning you use all their features, think about the data they have: searches, clicks, email content, images, location information, and everything else.

Through Google Ads, when you use a key word to search for something like running shoes, the marketing departments of these shoe companies are all like, "Pick me! Pick me!" The companies with the highest bids are placed at the top of your search results. So, you don't necessarily get the *best* response first, but you see a list of businesses that paid the most money to be seen by you. Then, when you actually click on say, Shoes R Us, Shoes R Us again throws a few coins at Google as a thank you for featuring them. You feel like you're in control since you got to choose to click on the ad. However, Google was in control of what ads you saw where in your search results. The motivation of that placement was getting the marketers' money, not serving you.

Influencers

By definition, influencers are people online who influence our thoughts, feelings, choices, and purchases. We may follow them for any number of reasons. Perhaps we like what they stand for, we admire their style, we are intrigued by their lifestyle, we love to hate them, we want their advice on hard topics, and the list goes on. When influencers invite us into their lives, it makes us feel like we know them, are connected to them, and trust them. This is especially true when they are mixed into our feeds with "ordinary" friends that we have real relationships with. We often feel loyal to influencers in a way that we don't with companies or even celebrities.

Because of this relationship, and massive followings, brands have come to realize that influencers are more powerful advertising than any stand-alone ad. In fact, one study suggested that 74 percent of consumers decide what to buy based on social media posts. So, brands are partnering with influencers to advertise to us. Even though we may believe we don't drink the Kool-Aid, thinking, *I wouldn't buy something just because this person said it's awesome*, we do. And it's making a tremendous amount of money for the brands and the influencers. Top YouTubers like Lilly Singh, Preston Arsement, or Ryan Kaji (ten years old, y'all) make between $10 and $30 million in a year.

I'm not saying don't watch or follow your faves anymore. (Remember, this book is not about what you should or shouldn't do. That's up to you.) I just think it can be helpful to keep it in the back of our minds that while yes, that watch is really cool, the person wearing it isn't doing so just because they think it's cool. They are doing it because they think it's cool *and* it's making them a crap-ton of money. They are doing it because they are making a brand an equally large amount of money.

And then there's Google AdSense. Google AdSense is a program that works by scouring a website and then choosing advertisements that fit into the content of that site and the user accessing it. Like, if I try to click on a magazine site reviewing the best running shoes of 2022, in addition to their content, I see an ad for specific brands of shoes sprinkled throughout the recommendations (and likely shoe brands I've looked at before). It can be so mixed in that it is hard to tell what part is the magazine recommendation and what part is the advertisement (very clever). If you do so happen to click on an ad on the site (on purpose or not), both the website *and* Google get a cut of the profits. So Google is integrating the optimal—for them—ads into web pages so that certain companies are most likely to make money.

Our user experience of this search engine is that we decide what we search for, click on, and buy. We do have that control on the front end. However, on the back end, Google (in cahoots with the marketing arms of thousands of companies) decides what to show us, where to place it, and how to show it to us. And the way they make those choices is based on an incredible database of information they already have on us designed to make us most likely to spend money. We simply aren't as in control as we feel like we are.

Maybe you are sitting there like, *Whoa.* Maybe you are sitting there like, *So what?* The bottom line is this: it benefits us to remember that we are on one side of the screen, doing our thing. Yet there is a whole network of very smart people and artificial intelligence on the other side, working really hard to make sure the thing we are doing makes them money. They are master manipulators. And we are all falling for it.

CHAPTER 3

Myth-Busting and Fact-Finding

"Technology's Impact on Health: Anxiety, Depression, and Social Network Use"

"Smartphones Are Making Us Stupid—and May Be a 'Gateway Drug'"

"Mobile Addiction Growing at an Alarming Rate"

Yowzah. While the media is passing down messages like these, it is easy to react quickly and fearfully. Parents may overreact to a headline without reading the full article or the original study. And writers might be reacting to a single study instead of critically reading it and considering how it fits into the context of other studies. The truth is, many headlines and articles oversimplify issues to the point where they end up creating and perpetuating myths and half-truths. When you are making decisions about your well-being, it helps to understand the truth about some of these clickbait messages. Let's explore a few statements, digging into the research to decide whether these alarming headlines are myths, facts, or some combination of both.

Myth or Fact 1: Technology causes depression and anxiety.

Here we have three headlines that paint a stark picture. Should we take them at face value?

"Can't Fight This Feeling: Technology and Teen Anxiety"

"The Risk of Teen Depression and Suicide Is Linked to Smartphone Use, Study Says"

"Technology Triggers Teen Depression"

If you were to just read the headlines without a critical eye, you might decide to throw your phone into the ocean and never look back. While many headlines imply that smartphone or technology use is causing mental health disorders, very few studies are actually stating exactly that. And just as with social media and video game platforms, many blogs, magazines, and other content creators are relying on clickbait headlines to draw you in. They need a standout headline so you will read their article and . . . *Whoa! Those are the shoes I want on sale! Gotta go. . . .*

So, does digital technology cause anxiety and depression? The answer is that it's complicated. Let's pick this question apart a little. When an alarming headline comes out, look at what the study the article is written about is actually measuring. Is everyone using their technology and phones the same way? Are gaming, social media, and YouTube video browsing all mashed up together? Does it matter? How much time do people who are dealing with these specific mental health issues spend on devices? Does one cause the other or are they simply linked? A headline, and often even an article itself, flattens out much of the complexity that may have been a part of the original study, usually to alarm you and make you click. This is both effective and misleading.

Recently, researchers have been combing through all the studies on these topics, and they are *still* reaching wildly different conclusions. Candice Odgers, a professor at the University of California Irvine, reviewed forty studies and found no evidence of a link between social media use and anxiety and depression. Jeff Hancock, who founded the Stanford Social Media Lab, came to a similar conclusion around phone use and well-being after reviewing 226 studies. On the flip side, a research team from the Hospital for Sick Children in Toronto reached the conclusion that there is enough evidence about technology and mental health that we should be limiting use. Jean Twenge's research kicked off this whole argument after she concluded in her 2017 book *iGen* that teen rates of suicide, depression, and anxiety were directly correlated to the rise of cell phone use. However, as we critical thinkers know, correlation does not equal causation. Furthermore, Andrew Przybylski, director of research at the Oxford Internet Institute, University of Oxford, was able to show that *eating potatoes* had the same effect on adolescent well-being as screen use. Yes, potatoes.

So who is right? I'm not sure. I told you it's complex.

Scientific Literacy

To read the news effectively, especially about the newest psychological study, we all need to keep a few things in mind about research studies.

First and foremost, it is very difficult to prove anything with a single study in the social sciences (think: human behavior). A study should be replicated repeatedly to confirm that its findings are accurate for a more general set of conditions. Together, a group of studies may start to get us closer to the truth. A meta-analysis, or a synthesis of multiple studies in a field, can be more helpful.

Second, check out the sampling. How many people were involved in the study? Does the group of people sampled represent the population as a whole, or was it one specific group only? For example, if a study has only white teen boys as participants, we cannot necessarily say whatever was found in the study is true for young women or BIPOC teens.

Third, people don't often publish studies with inconclusive results because no one cares about those studies. We want results! So we are naturally biased toward studies that prove *something interesting happened*! But we don't always know the full extent of the research.

Fourth, the word *correlation* means something different than *causation*. Something may be related, or correlated, but that does not mean it is the cause of something else (though we may be quick to say so). Some correlations we draw conclusions about are so small that they are essentially meaningless—but that doesn't stop us from trying.

I wish we could count on all journalists to frame breaking news items in these terms, but in an era of fast-paced news cycles and catchy headlines, we must rely on our own critical-thinking skills more than ever.

My conclusion is that if you are struggling with a mental health condition, it is worth considering how your technology use may exacerbate (or alleviate) your symptoms. Just as food, exercise, and stress impact our well-being, our technology use does too. But how and why and when? The jury is still out.

This is where mindfulness comes in. Rather than seeking answers only outside of ourselves, what if we also investigate how we are doing? Do we feel anxious or depressed? Are those feelings exacerbated by any particular activities? Soothed? What happens if we limit or eliminate certain habits for a set period of time? This research into our own experience will reveal the most important data to help us make healthy decisions for ourselves.

So, does technology cause depression and anxiety?
Technology use is certainly linked to anxiety and depression, and it may even cause it, but it's definitely more complicated than those headlines suggest. It all depends on the kind of technology, length of time, and the person using it. The most important thing is to consider how it may be impacting *you.*

Myth or Fact 2: Using technology causes stress.

Of course, technology *can* cause stress. Just about anything can.

Stress happens when your mind interprets a situation as overwhelming and beyond your capacity to handle it. Your body enters a "fight, flight, or freeze" state, which means it floods with hormones such as adrenaline and cortisol to protect you from imminent danger. This is useful if we are about to be attacked, run over by a car, or burned on a stove. We need to quickly move our bodies to safety or defend ourselves. And that body movement actually helps flush all that adrenaline and cortisol out of our systems. Ideally, we'd follow it with a long period of recovery in which we rest, maybe take a bubble bath, read some fluff magazine, and soothe our systems.

So what happens when that danger starts with a nasty Instagram comment, then a zombie that has jumped out from the side of your screen, then an argument between two YouTube stars happening right before your eyes, then whatever happens in the next click that your body perceives as threatening? Your fight, flight, or freeze response is not so helpful when it comes to technology, because there's nothing to physically fight or run from. So each of these little stressors creates a reaction in our nervous system, and when we are rapidly giving ourselves little jolts of adrenaline all day, we cannot process it. Our bodies are able to handle small stressors spaced out throughout the day when there is time to return to a baseline. They can even handle big stressors that occur once in a while, if we process them. However, our systems are not built to be flooded with hormones for long periods of time without relief. We need time for our nervous systems to return to a relaxed state.

According to psychiatrist Victoria Dunckley, simply viewing highly stimulating shows with rapidly changing colors, lights, and sounds can send us into a state of hyperarousal she has dubbed "electronic screen syndrome," in which we feel jittery and reactive. If we watch a lot of such media or play a lot of these kinds of video games, and we have no downtime in our day to move or decompress, we never fully relax, and our nervous system never fully calms down. Over time, this can mean we are more reactive to other things in our lives, because our nervous systems never really settle back to baseline, and we are basically on edge, physically ready to protect ourselves from danger.

We know that screen use can certainly cause stress. Here's where the story again gets complicated. What if I am just looping videos of cute kittens cuddling elephants or ASMR videos? (ASMR videos show people whispering, chewing gum, or making other sounds that can produce an autonomous sensory meridian response—ASMR—or pleasant tingly sensations in its listeners.) What if I am just mindlessly playing Snake? What if I get up and move my body every so often? Probably a different story, right? It is important to consider *what you are doing* on the screen as well as how much time you are spending.

Our Sweet Li'l Ancient Nervous System

We've got this nervous system that has served us really well over time, but it has not adapted well to modern stressors. The nervous system includes the brain, spinal cord, and network of nerves throughout the body that communicate and respond to the environment, often without our conscious input.

When we are calm, we exist in a parasympathetic state, or "rest and digest mode," because our body is at ease. Actions that might support you being in this mode include:

- Swinging in a hammock on a warm summer day
- Falling into bed after winning a championship game
- Being silly with your best friends

If we think of the parasympathetic state as gently easing on brakes and settling down, the sympathetic state is like slamming on the gas pedal. In this "fight, flight, or freeze" mode, our nervous system senses danger and prepares to save the self by any means necessary. Things that might trigger you into this mode include:

- A giant moose appearing on a trail in front of you
- A car coming within inches of your precious body as you're about to step onto the road
- A pop quiz
- Seeing an Instagram post of all your friends at a party you weren't invited to

The sympathetic state is triggered when the lower region of your brain detects a threat, then short-circuits the rest of the brain and floods the body with preparatory hormones to save yourself!

Let's also consider what you are *not* doing when you are on a screen. Are you not getting into nature, which has been proven to lower stress hormones? Are you not exercising, discharging some of that adrenaline and cortisol? Are you not snuggling up with your kitten and soaking in the cuddle hormone? Are you not meeting with your friends face-to-face? Are you not sleeping? We need to balance our screen use with other bodily needs, so consider what doesn't get done when you are glued to your tech. We need stress reduction activities that help us reset. Technology is not always the best way to do that.

So, does using technology make people stressed?
Technology can contribute to your stress, but again, it depends on what you are doing and how much. If you are experiencing a lot of stress, consider the ways you use your tech, and think about whether changing your tech use could help you manage that stress.

Myth or Fact 3: Using technology makes people dumb.

Our brains have this amazing neuroplasticity to them. That is, the structures physically change and rewire through learning and experiences. Whatever you do on technology trains your mind to form stronger connections between neurons and do that thing better. If you are skipping around quickly, perusing articles, and skimming, you will become a better skimmer. If you play fast-paced video games, you will probably get better at paying attention in high-stimulation environments. In fact, a 2018 study suggested that people who play video games are better at screening for important information and ignoring distractions in fast-paced environments. However, this practice may be less useful if you are trying to read *Moby Dick,* understand a dense research paper, or write the next great American novel. Basically, the way your brain engages with technology makes it easier for your brain to pay attention in that particular way. But it can also make it harder for your brain to pay attention in other ways, if you are not training it to do other kinds of thinking.

Again, think about it: what are you *not* doing when you're playing video games? Are you not doing your homework, reading difficult or complex text, or pondering big life questions? Sustained, intensive attention is built by working through complex math problems, reading difficult literature, and using your brain for more complicated and difficult tasks. A study done on young teens used an MRI to map out their brains. The researchers found that teens who read more showed more connectivity in areas of the brain related to language and cognitive control (this is our ability to set a goal and work toward it), and those who spent more time on screens showed less connectivity. Brain rewiring at work. Notably, this study did not get into what areas of the brain were strengthened from screen use. Bias much?

Nicholas Carr wrote a fascinating book called *The Shallows: What the Internet Is Doing to Our Brains.* In it, he talks about how our brains were not actually made to read. That was a skill we developed over time, with practice. That's right, we aren't all born good or bad readers (though some neurodiversity clearly makes reading more difficult for some people than others). Reading is a skill that must be *practiced* because it is really hard for our brains. And I would argue that reading is important. It is one of the ways we stay connected to our past, learn to empathize with others, and communicate deeply meaningful ideas across time and space. It is how we stay up to date with current events, and it can be a medium to exchange ideas with people on the other side of the world.

How are we to know the right ratio of the different modes of thinking? While I am sure someone out there will try to sell us some program that claims to know this, we can't possibly know. Each particular brain is too complex to make up a hard and fast rule. If you are finding you have a hard time paying attention to more complex tasks, that's a good cue that you may need to spend more time doing them (painful as it may be). Just because something is difficult doesn't mean you can't do it.

So, does using technology make people dumb?

Technology does not inherently make us dumber. But what we are doing while on our technology—and what we aren't doing—absolutely impacts the way our brains are wired and what kinds of thinking we are most capable of. If you are spending many of your waking hours scrolling and gaming, you may be more agile but less able to pay attention in a sustained way and do deeper thinking. We may want to consider what kinds of thinking we need to improve and make sure we build time into our lives for that.

Myth or Fact 4: Reading paper books and articles is better than reading them on a screen.

Researchers have been studying how our learning and understanding is affected when we read from a screen as compared to reading a physical book or paper to try to understand whether it really matters.

Virginia Clinton-Lisell, assistant professor of education at the University of North Dakota, looked at all the studies she could find comparing reading from paper to reading from screens. Reviewing thirty-three studies, she found that we do tend to learn somewhat better from paper than screens. Why? Well, the jury is still out. Some people think it's because we read too fast on screens. Others say it's simply because most people still prefer reading from paper. Still others think maybe it's because we don't actually use all the cool learning features you could embed in an online text that would help us get it. Clinton-Lisell thinks it could be it's because we are overconfident in our understanding, so we don't read as carefully. We don't have solid answers about why we are overconfident, but there is some evidence that it may be because we are used to reading screen text (text messages, emails, BuzzFeed articles) less carefully. When we are asked to read something more complex on a screen, we might to fail to slow down and give it the time and attention it needs.

I can say for myself that I really prefer a physical book or printed article. I notice more easily when my mind has wandered, and I can go back and find where I stopped reading and started daydreaming about a hot fudge brownie sundae (*mmmm . . . yummy*). I like the way a book feels in my hands, and the physical act of turning pages helps prompt me to recognize if I am focused on the book or not.

As for trying to learn from a nonfiction article, I find I don't remember as easily if I am reading something on a screen. I really like to write all over articles when I'm reading, and I can't do that if I am skimming something on the computer. I find I have an especially hard time online because all the banners, hypertexts, and pop-ups are distractions that take brain power to ignore. Being on a screen also means feeling a constant draw toward easier activities. For example, right now, going on TikTok would be easier than trying to write this book. Part of my mind must continue to resist that urge that gets stronger the more I want to stop writ— . . . be back in a few.

So, is reading paper books and articles better than reading them online?

Research seems to suggest there may be some benefit to reading hard copies over screen versions, but it's not a huge difference and could just be about where you are most comfortable reading. It's a worthwhile investigation for yourself. Do you notice a difference? Start paying attention to how well you understand and focus while reading on different mediums. If you are trying to read articles online, do you notice part of your brain trying to ignore the scrolling videos and flashy

Journal Prompt

How does learning about some of the research around technology use impact the ways you would like to use technology?

images? What does it physically feel like to hold a book as compared to an e-reader? Do you have a preference? At the end of the day, any reading is better than no reading (see page 63), so maybe you choose how you read based on how much you need to take away from a text. Celebrity gossip can probably be gleaned from your phone. Reading for school may be best read printed out or from a physical book.

Myth or Fact 5: Handwriting is better than typing.

Researchers all agree that the process of writing by hand is very different from typing. Handwriting is a complex physical process that requires a lot of you, the writer, and forces you to slow down. Typing is as simple and physically easy as pressing a key. While typing feels like a more efficient way of taking notes, and indeed, we tend to write down more information, research suggests we may actually learn more if we take handwritten notes. This is thought to be because we tend to type word-for-word, whereas we process and reword information more when we write it down. That pre-processing that we do before we get it to the page allows us to integrate it more fully into our schema.

That said, the speed, ease, and convenience of typing should not be discounted. Maybe what would be most helpful is to think about the kind of writing we are trying to do, and then choose longhand or typing based on our goals.

Take journaling, for example. If your purpose is just to jot some notes down quickly and easily, it might make sense to keep a digital journal. This may also be a better form if you want to have something at hand all the time: your phone is likely already there, whereas a paper journal is another object to remember. However, if you are hoping to have a more creative and free-form journaling experience that allows you to mind map, draw, and write, having a physical journal might be a better option. Physical journals force us to activate our minds in a way that digital journals don't. We have to slow down just to get the ideas out, and when we're done, we have a record of all those thoughts, including the parts we cross out, insert, and reword. It is a fuller documentation.

The other benefit to a physical journal is that it doesn't distract us with other things that might be easier or more fun. Games and social media may become irresistible as we are trying to work out something uncomfortable or difficult. *I could keep trying to figure out this fight that just happened with my so-called friends, but it'd feel a whole lot better to pop over to Instagram and scroll mindlessly for the next thirty minutes.* Staying with and reflecting on our life experiences has value, and we don't want to always distract ourselves to the point that we don't feel hard feelings and explore difficult thoughts.

So, is handwriting better than typing?
It depends on your goals. Writing longhand may give us a slower, more creative experience and help us retain information by processing it as we go. Typing is quick, easy, and accessible, and it may be better for on-the-go recording and when we want to capture information word for word.

Myth or Fact 6: People can multitask just as well as they can single task.

We often multitask with our devices, completing homework while receiving text messages from friends and scrolling through Instagram. And we really, truly believe we are good at it—like, studies show we think this. But it turns out, our brains cannot process two things at one time. Instead, we quickly switch between tasks, but every time we try to turn our attention back to the task at hand, it takes the brain a while to catch up. Experts say it can take up to twenty minutes to delve back into a task that requires deeper thinking! Can you imagine what this means for homework?

I'm writing my essay, I'm writing my essay . . .
Hear ding.
Read text message.
Respond.
Write to other friend about text message.
Notice notification from Instagram.
Check notification on Instagram.
Like cute photo.
And we're back. *Okay, essay. Wait, what? What was I talking about? Okay, now I am going to go back and reread a few sentences. And . . . hmm. Well, maybe something like this?*
Twenty minutes later we may be back in the flow, just in time for . . . Snap notification!

You see how this can spiral?

And what if we are not trying to write but trying to study and take information into our brains? As Nicholas Carr tells us in a short, animated YouTube video *What the Internet Is Doing to Our Brains*, when we study, we put little nuggets of info into our short-term memory area. Later on, those nuggets get bumped into our long-term memory as we connect them to other information we have already stored.

If you interrupt that process from short-term to long-term storage with a distraction (text ding!), your memory will bump out that bit of info, and you'll have to restart the whole learning process again.

A lot of the work we are asked to do for school is challenging. If we keep switching our attention back and forth between homework and the more fun thing—a YouTube video, a text chain, TikTok videos—it makes the homework that much harder. It means we will be less efficient, less accurate, and less in-depth with our work. So we have to decide if we'd rather sit down and get it done or half pay attention to multiple things. (Okay, okay, I have an obvious bias here. But maybe you'll decide you'd really rather spend a little more time if it means you can watch *Finding Nemo* in the background.)

So, can people multitask just as well as they can single task?

Hard and fast on this one: No. We simply cannot multitask as well as we can tackle one thing at a time. That doesn't mean we should never do it. But if we are trying to learn something new or share our genius ideas with others, we probably should set aside the distractions and give our full attention to our work.

Myth or Fact 7: People can be addicted to technology.

Fifty percent of teens feel addicted to their mobile devices.
—Common Sense Media, 2016

Forty-five percent of parents feel personally addicted to their mobile device, an 18-point increase since 2016. For children, 39 percent feel addicted themselves, an 11-point decline since 2016.
—Common Sense Media, 2019

Can you be addicted to your device? It depends on who you ask. Seriously, there's no scientific consensus on this subject yet. (Are you detecting a trend here?)

We can consider the arguments for and against and think about where we might fall. Usually when people say they are "addicted" to technology, they mean it more colloquially than scientifically. When we say we are addicted to technology, we might mean that we feel like it's running our lives and we don't want to be without it. This doesn't necessarily mean that a psychologist would diagnose us with an addiction and discuss treatment options.

In what ways is technology addictive? An addiction is defined as a brain disease that shows itself when someone compulsively uses a substance or keeps doing a behavior, despite harmful consequences. Just using a phone a lot does not meet the description of an addiction in the clinical sense. But if you find you keep staring at your screen even though it's getting in the way of your life, that might be a sign of an addiction.

Let's take a look at some of the American Psychiatric Association's criteria for what interference in your life might mean in terms of gaming (but can easily be applied to other activities). Do any of these apply to you?

- Constantly think about video games and nothing else
- Feel anxious or angry when you can't play them
- Need to keep playing more and more to feel satisfied
- Feel out of control and like you can't stop
- Lie to other people about how much you are playing
- No longer interested in doing things away from a screen (such as hanging out with friends or family or going for a walk)
- Keep playing even though you can see that it makes you feel bad

- Use games to escape from difficult feelings
- Have lost something really important to you because you've been gaming

I'm not here to diagnose you with an addiction. Again, only a trained psychologist can do that. And some psychologists don't think that screen behavior itself is the problem—they argue that people who use their electronics excessively are actually struggling with other disorders and using the computer or phone as a coping mechanism. That said, awareness of these clues about unhealthy consequences of our technology use may be the first step in realizing if and when you need to make changes or seek help.

Technology Addiction Support

Because ever-present digital technology is a newer phenomenon, we are only just starting to understand how to support people who may have developed addictive habits around screens. Some psychologists and social workers are starting to specialize in this area, and programs are cropping up to help people deal with internet addiction. ReSTART, one of the first residential addiction treatment programs in the United States, supports teens who have experienced a decline in their quality of life because of excessive technology use.

While the United States does not yet formally recognize technology as an addiction, countries including China and South Korea recognize internet addiction and treat it as such. The World Health Organization recognizes that excessive internet use has negative health implications and has added gaming disorder to the International Classification of Diseases.

So, can people get addicted to technology?

Being on your phone a ton? Not necessarily an addiction. There are certain criteria that define an addiction, and in the United States, tech addiction is not yet a clinical diagnosis. However, keep in mind that just because you can't be diagnosed as "addicted" in this country doesn't mean technology use can't be harmful. Start paying attention to your habits and how they are affecting you. If you do find your tech usage is interfering with your life, get help with kicking some of those habits.

Myth or Fact 8: Technology messes with your sleep.

The biggest technology problem for most young people I talk with is that they are not sleeping well. They stay up too late on their phones or playing video games instead of going to bed. This seems to match a general nationwide trend. A 2019 Common Sense Media study found that one-third of teens woke up to check their mobile devices in the middle of the night. Furthermore, nearly three-fourths of them check their phones up to thirty minutes before falling asleep.

The problem is not just about replacing sleep with technology time. Even using screens during the day can affect our sleep cycles at night. The bright light disrupts our bodies' release of melatonin, a chemical that tells our bodies to sleep. This disruption prevents our bodies from going into really deep sleep. That deep sleep is called REM, short for rapid eye movement, and it's the sleep that leaves us feeling rested. While blue light is often to blame, even shifting into a more orange tint can keep you up. That's why we often hear that we should be off our screens an hour or two before bed. But even just being on the screen a lot throughout the day can affect sleep and lead to sleep deprivation issues.

The Teenage Brain

Your brain is in a fascinating stage of development. The changes happening now actually help you move away from your family, and you have more drive to take risks than at any other period in your life! But you are also in more danger of developing addictions. How does that work? A few things are at play.

All brains have a chemical called dopamine. Remember dopamine? It is released when we like something, and it makes us feel good. As a teen, your brain has less dopamine in its neutral state than when you're an adult. But you also get a much bigger dopamine spike as a teen when you do something that is pleasant for you than an adult would. Basically, this spike makes you want to do the thing over and over and over, more than an adult would, because you're getting a bigger hit. You can see how you might start to crave that bump because it feels so good when that chemical is released.

Also, your prefrontal cortex, which helps with impulse control and thoughtful decision-making, doesn't fully develop until you're in your mid-twenties. This is not a knock against you. Again, it actually makes you less afraid to try new things. However, it also means your choices can more easily become compulsive and out of your control than if you were an adult. So, you need to take extra care around any potentially addictive substance or behavior, because it's just plain easier for you to get hooked.

So, does technology mess with your sleep?

Technology absolutely can mess with your sleep. (I suspect most of you know that from personal experience, right?) If you feel well rested, sleep like a rock, and are clocking the recommended hours, you probably don't have to worry about it. But if you're walking around like a zombie all day or struggling to get to sleep or stay asleep, it's important to consider tech as one aspect of your sleep-better plan. See if you can start noticing your energy levels throughout the day. Though it is normal to have natural dips and

SLEEP

Most teens function best if they sleep between eight and ten hours every night. Where are you on that spectrum?

Not getting enough sleep can really mess you up. When you aren't sleeping, it's harder to concentrate the next day. Your grades can suffer. It's more likely that you'll get into a car accident. Lack of sleep can cause and exacerbate depression and anxiety. It can create inflammation in the body. It messes with your hormones. And generally, you just feel like a pile of poop.

Part of the struggle (and the struggle is real) is that teen body-clock timing and school-day timing don't match up very well. Your body tends to release melatonin, a sleep-inducing hormone, later in the night than adults, and keeps you sleeping later into the morning . . . about two hours later, in fact. So, seven and eight o'clock school start times really put a damper on the natural rhythms of your body. In fact, the American Academy of Pediatrics recommends that start times for middle and high schools be no earlier than eight thirty a.m.!

rebounds, if you are perpetually dog-tired, it likely means you ought to try something different.

Myth or Fact 9: Technology use messes with people's health.

A fair amount has been written about how technology use can impact our bodies. As with any other impact, it depends on the amount of time we spend on devices and what we are doing. If I play Wii Fit with a balance board for three hours a day, that will obviously have

While the ol' school-start-time debate may be raging above your head and feel out of your control, some habits *are* within your control.

TIPS AND TRICKS FOR A BETTER NIGHT'S SLEEP

- Go to sleep at night and wake up in the morning around the same time every day.
- Use wind-down routines, such as warm showers or reading in bed.
- Exercise regularly.
- Limit caffeine, especially in the afternoon.
- Keep your bedroom dark and cool.
- If you can, keep your bedroom a space only for sleeping. (Or at the very least, stop pulling your laptop into bed with you!)
- And, of course, practice limiting your device use, especially at night. (Consider getting an alarm clock to use instead of your phone.)

a very different impact than if I am curled up on the couch, hunched over my phone, for that same amount of time. So what are some of the recorded physical impacts?

Computer vision syndrome. Also known as *digital eye strain*, this condition includes a host of symptoms that come from staring at our screens for too long. Symptoms include eye strain, headaches, blurred vision, dry eyes, and neck and shoulder pain. We can combat some of these concerns by blinking, positioning the screen away from glare, sitting with upright posture, and taking regular breaks.

Text neck. Our spines have a natural curve, with the upper cervical spine curving in a gentle *C* up the neck. Consider what happens when you look at your phone. Your cervical spine flattens, and your shoulders tend to hunch forward. Should you stay in this position for a long time, you might start to experience muscle tension or headaches. Just doing things like holding the phone up to eye level and periodically stretching the spine can help alleviate some of this body misalignment.

Sedentary lifestyle. This boils down to what we are NOT doing more than what we are doing. Now, if you're a *Dance Dance Revolution* master, this is probably not as much of a problem for you. But if you're spending a ton of time sitting on your derriere, your body doesn't get much chance to move. The thing is, many teens are already not moving a lot because of long hours at school. (Come on, school, get with the program! Our bodies need to move!) Regardless, research shows that those who use technology the most tend to move their bodies the least, which has all sorts of health effects, like raising your blood pressure (not so good for the heart). The American Academy of Pediatrics recommends at least sixty minutes of activity most days, with muscle- and bone-strengthening activities three or more days per week. So, if you find yourself running around on a screen more than running around your neighborhood, it might be worth occasionally trading in your controller for a pair of walking shoes.

So, does technology use mess with people's health?

Spending a lot of time on your device can certainly affect your eyes, posture, and the amount of movement you get (which has all sorts of health implications). Start investigating your own personal balance. Are you still getting those sixty-plus minutes of exercise in your day? Do you generally feel healthy, energized, and strong? Do you take regular breaks to stretch your eyes and spine while using technology? It's worth paying attention to our physical health and considering how technology impacts it.

Technology Can Help Improve Physical Health

Technology can actually help us improve our health in a lot of ways. It can help us find motivation, instruction, and inspiration! If you are looking for support in these areas, consider any of the resources below.

Step counters Certain phones and watches can actually track the number of steps you take each day. Some people also use a watch or fitness tracking device that can connect with their phone. In the fitness community, there's a prevailing belief that ten thousand steps per day is the key to health and well-being. But one helpful way to use these tools is to find out what your baseline is. Then see if you can best yourself over time. If you're only getting in three or four thousand steps each day, challenge yourself to hit five thousand.

Water trackers If our bodies are made up of about 60 percent water, you can see how having enough helps keep all our systems functioning. I have definitely experienced headaches and stomach issues when I don't drink enough water. Doctors suggest adolescents take in seven to fourteen cups of liquid each day to maintain health. But that's not just water—even some of your food (like a juicy apple) counts. If you struggle to get enough liquids down, some really fun apps out there can encourage you to drink water. One of my favorites that my students introduced to me has you take care of a virtual plant through your water consumption. The more water you drink, the more the plant grows. (Apt metaphor, no?)

Nutrition suggestions Figuring out what to eat can be tricky. While our bodies give us clear signals about when we are hungry and full (which we may only notice if we are not on our screens while eating, ahem), sometimes it can be hard to figure out *what* to eat. The US Department of Agriculture and the National Institutes of Health both have basic guidelines to help get you started. From there, you can find endless websites for recipes, cooking videos, and even chef influencers.

Workout suggestions Millions of options are available for finding workout suggestions. If you are completely sedentary, you may look for easy workouts that get you off the couch. If you are already an athlete, you may search for workouts that match your sport of choice. I have found apps that provide inspiration for my body-weight workouts at home, weighted gym workouts when I want to get stronger, and training advice when I am working toward running a longer race. You can also search for these on YouTube or social media. Just be an informed consumer and make sure the messaging is about health and not size. Smaller is not better.

Yoga and mobility videos I love being able to turn on a fifteen-minute video at the end of the day and have someone else tell me what to do. YouTube is full of yoga videos. Just make sure you find someone who matches your fitness level. Lots of yoga does not involve twisting yourself into a pretzel and can still help your body feel open and strong.

Inspiration Before we launch into this aspect of health, it feels really important to get clear on what is actually healthy versus what we are told is healthy. Remember, many companies want you to feel bad about yourself so that they can "fix" you when you buy their product. And they even use social media influencers to promote the idea that you need to change. So we need to be careful about consuming media that actually helps us feel strong and healthy versus media that promotes being skinny, super muscular, or "hot." The messages and images we take in from our technology can deeply and subconsciously impact how we feel about our bodies.

If you follow a fitness influencer, notice their messaging. If they are trying to sell you some product, or tell you that you need to lose five pounds to go to the beach, it's probably time to drop 'em. Even if you don't believe that junk, it makes its way into your mind and can create a toxic body image.

Instead, when searching for inspiration—whether it be on social media, through videos, or in articles—find people who are truly promoting health and positive self-image. Find some badass athletes to follow who show how having a strong and well-nourished body enables them to achieve! As a runner, one of my favorite follows is a woman named Hillary Gerardi, who lives overseas and competes in intense mountain races. Think about what sport inspires you (you don't even have to play it) and try giving athletes in those fields a follow. Athletes can help remind us that our bodies are for moving and doing cool stuff, not for looking at.

CHAPTER 4

What Is Mindfulness and Why Is It Such a Big Deal?

Perhaps you've seen images of star basketball player LeBron James on the sideline of his game, eyes closed and taking deep breaths, or heard the Seattle Seahawks coach share that meditation was a part of their practice routine after their Super Bowl win in 2014. Maybe you've heard the hype about Google's in-house mindfulness program. Or perhaps an aunt, friend, mentor, teacher, or drama coach has mentioned they are using mindfulness to help them be less stressed. At this point in your life, you've likely at least heard about this idea of mindfulness. It's everywhere.

So, what, exactly, are we talking about here? While it can be difficult to define, at its simplest, mindfulness is paying attention to the present moment with curiosity and compassion. As it turns out, you can notice lots of things at any given moment: the smell of freshly cut grass, a twinge in your shoulder, a swirling worry with an accompanying stomach clenching. When we tune in to our environment using our senses, we may find everything externally seems a bit more vivid, as thoughts and emotions fade into the background. Paying attention to our bodies, particularly at points that connect with the ground, can have a settling effect. If we are more conscious of bodily sensations throughout the day, we can more easily and quickly recognize when we have an unmet need (*I am finding my brother extra annoying right now because I'm hangry, not because he's doing anything wrong*). By being aware of external cues, we can stay connected to the reality of this moment, even if it gets a little messy inside. By being aware of our mind states—emotions, moods, and thoughts—we can start to see clearly how we tick, and how our patterns and habits impact us—for better and worse.

And y'all, there's a lot going on in there. All the time. For everyone. As a species, our minds tend to be all over the place: to the past, future, and back again in five seconds flat. Our ability to think about things that already happened, or things that haven't happened yet, is incredibly useful for reflecting and planning. However, it is also incredibly exhausting when we are just trying to get some sleep. Mindfulness teaches us to notice where our mind is. It gives us tools for refocusing the mind and practices for softening the inner narrator, who for many of us, can be a big jerk.

So, what are the benefits of learning this mindfulness stuff? Some promising research has focused on young people, who learn mindfulness as an intervention taught by highly trained teachers. These studies have found the following results.

- **Less perceived stress.** Mindfulness can help people recognize that some stressors may not be as significant as they thought, and so people react less strongly to them.
- **Less emotional reactivity.** Mindfulness can help folks keep their heads on straight and make a plan rather than turning into a stress puddle on the floor. This might help that pile of homework seem less overwhelming.

- **Fewer depressive symptoms.** Some people found that over time, as they practiced mindfulness, they felt more motivated and connected to their lives.
- **Fewer difficult, intrusive thoughts.** Intrusive thoughts are unwanted thoughts, images, impulses, and urges. For example, maybe you keep thinking about that "stupid" thing you said in class yesterday, and replaying and replaying it in your mind, over and over and over. With mindfulness, folks can start to interrupt those thoughts by noticing them and trying to banish them: *Aha! There you are again! Scram!* Then they can shift their focus to some anchor in the present moment, like music playing or sunshine or a breeze.
- **Better grades and academic performance.** This makes sense, right? If someone can better focus and react less emotionally, they are set up to be more successful in school.
- **More mindful attention.** People can better notice when they are carried away by a distraction and wake back up to this moment. *Oh, wait, here I am!*
- **Better self-image.** Compassion practices invite people to work on being kind to themselves with mindfulness. This helps them notice when their inner critic is raging and know they don't have to believe everything that critic is thinking.

Who came up with this ingenious system? you might wonder. Mindfulness has a rich history, impossible to fully explain in a few paragraphs. My personal understanding of mindfulness has been built through many different teachers, traditions, and experiences. For me, it started with an academic understanding of the habits of mind through psychology and Buddhism courses. It was when I started training with Mindful Schools that I found I was really able to bring awareness into my daily life. My personal practice has been deeply illuminated through practice and retreat with teachers from the Insight Meditation Society (IMS) and coursework within the mindfulness-based stress reduction (MBSR) framework. My understanding of mindfulness can be attributed to a number of different lineages, which I then made sense of in my own life.

Indeed, the mindfulness we see in the West today has been part of many religious and cultural practices for thousands of years, though it is most strongly associated with Siddhartha Gautama and his teachings of Buddhism in about 500 BCE in what is present-day Nepal. Buddhist disciples carried his teachings forward and fanned out across the globe, and the understanding of these practices and their purpose evolved in the cultural contexts where these teachers landed. In the United States, a place that has always emphasized self-determination (we write our own story here!) and optimism (we can be whatever we want, if we just work hard enough for it), mindfulness is often taught as a way for individuals to learn more about their mind-body experience and how to be more at peace with themselves and others. Modern teachers I reference in my practice, including Sharon Salzberg, Jack Kornfield, and Joseph Goldstein, were integral to bringing mindfulness to the mainstream United States by helping Americans understand how these ancient traditions apply to their lives.

A man by the name of Jon Kabat-Zinn realized he could help people with chronic pain by using meditation techniques while on a retreat at IMS, where he envisioned the eight-week course now known as MBSR. This course, offered in hospitals and wellness centers, plunked mindfulness squarely into the medical field and gained scientific validity. Kabat-Zinn's research, combined with a growing interest in mental health, rocketed mindfulness to fame in the West, and the applications since then have been extensive. What started as a tiny mindful snowball in this country picked up speed and strength until it created a nationwide obsession. In fact, for better or worse, a $1.2 billion industry has built up around meditation.

These days, teachers including Rhonda Magee, Ruth King, Reverend angel Kyodo williams, and Lama Rod Owens are working to recenter the intended community-oriented ethical framework around mindfulness practice. The Buddha taught mindfulness not simply as a tool for self-help, but as a liberatory practice from suffering *for all beings*. These teachers have worked to come back to this idea that we are not separate from others but deeply interconnected, and our practice is in service of this understanding. As mindfulness practitioners, our role is to work to end that which causes suffering of all, including racism, sexism, homophobia, environmental destruction, and all other forms of oppression.

The Reach of Mindfulness in Society

Sports Mindfulness meditation has become a key part of winning sports teams' strategies to build mental endurance and clarity. Under Phil Jackson and George Mumford's joint guidance, the Chicago Bulls and Los Angeles Lakers incorporated mindfulness into their athletic pursuits and went on to rake in a combined eleven NBA championships. The Seattle Seahawks incorporated mindfulness coach and sports psychologist Michael Gervais into their training program, supporting their 2014 Super Bowl win.

Schools Mindful Schools, Mindfulness in Schools Project, Mindful Life, .b, and other organizations bring mindfulness to students, teachers, and schools around the world with the intention of improving well-being, cognitive skills, and academic performance.

Veterans The Mindful Veteran Project works with veterans to build mindfulness through workshops, phone pals, and service projects. This has proven helpful for those grappling with PTSD and other combat-related struggles.

How to Meditate

Many people practice mindfulness by meditating. That is, intentionally setting aside time to focus the mind, observe sensations in the body, or develop a kind attitude. Some people even go to weeklong retreats in silence (no phones allowed) to find stillness and understanding. (Yes, I am one of those people.) While meditation is often associated with images of people sitting cross-legged on a cushion, totally blissed out, it can actually be performed anywhere.

Companies Google has a "Search Inside Yourself" curriculum, General Mills adopted a seven-week mindfulness and meditation program, and even Goldman Sachs (an investment firm) has gotten in on the action by promoting a meditation app and hosting wellness seminars on the subject. Mindfulness in the workplace improves employee well-being, reduces absences, and increases productivity.

Therapy Some therapists introduce mindfulness-based cognitive therapy (MBCT) as a way of dealing with difficult thoughts and emotions. MBCT helps patients better understand their thoughts and emotional experiences.

Celebrities Oprah Winfrey; Trevor Noah; and Catherine, Duchess of Cambridge, are just a few celebrities who give a nod to mindfulness or meditation as part of their daily practice and way of being in the world. Oprah writes, "That outside world is constantly trying to convince you you're not enough. But you don't have to take the bait. Meditation, in whatever form you choose, helps you resist."

Meditation can be done while walking, lying down, or standing. In fact, not everyone who practices mindfulness even formally meditates. You can do it in as little as one breath: *Ah, here I am.*

Still don't think you can meditate? Let's explore how simple it can be!

Scan to listen.

Try this:

Notice the parts of your body that are connected to your seat or the ground. (Often, this is the feet, the bum, the backs of the legs.)

Sense that gentle downward pressure from gravity.

Be aware of any sensations in those parts of the body (such as temperature, tingling, or tightness).

Or try this:

Read the sentences below. But in between each line, close your eyes or look away from the page. (No, seriously. Do it.)

Tune in to the sounds around you. (pause)

Notice if there are sounds from nearby or far away. (pause)

There may be loud sounds or quiet, subtle sounds. (pause)

There may be pleasant and unpleasant sounds. (pause)

For a moment in time, just listen, and know that you are hearing. (pause)

Or this:

Focus on an entire breath: the rise and fall, the whole inhale, the pause at the top, the whole exhale, the pause at the bottom. Now try focusing on two breaths. And three . . .

See, you just did it! You practiced mindfulness. The foundation for this work is to just start noticing what's going on. Being present. Paying attention.

Diving into Meditation

MEDITATION APPS

Tons of apps out there can help you learn practices to cultivate mindful awareness. Here are just a few (and more are coming out each day).

- Stop, Breathe & Think
- Headspace
- Calm
- Smiling Mind
- Ten Percent Happier

TEEN MEDITATION RETREATS

Interested in trying a meditation retreat? Inward Bound Mindfulness Education (iBme) offers retreats on the East and West Coasts, as well as online options. Many retreats are five days long and, according to their website, involve "sitting and walking meditation, mindful movement, small group activities, workshops, and free time for socializing or resting." While these retreats involve periods of silence, there is also time for dialogue and fun! Fees are based on a sliding scale, and specific programs are available for LGBTQIA+ individuals and people of color.

Check out their website at ibme.com to learn more.

Please know that the intention with mindfulness is to be curious and compassionate. We want to invite ourselves to be curious, and even uncomfortable at times, but not overwhelmed. If you are ever experimenting with a practice and you suddenly find yourself overwhelmed with a big emotion or start shutting down, this is a sign that it's time to reorient to your space by looking around the room, shaking out your body, and doing something else. A compassionate response to our bodies telling us, "Hey, this is too much!" is to take a break. Know that it's always within your power to say no thanks to trying out any of these practices.

How to Be Mindful

Mindfulness does not have to involve meditation. You can practice being mindful simply by paying attention to the everyday things you are already doing. So often we are a million miles away mentally and our bodies just go on autopilot. Instead, we can be mindful by totally enjoying the feeling of falling into bed at night, noting the softness of our mattress and the coolness of our sheets. We can be mindful by fully listening when our earbuds are in, noticing the rise and fall of melodies and harmonies of our favorite songs. Even noticing the way a particular beat or line changes the way our bodies feel is a moment of full awareness. We can be mindful while eating breakfast, actually tasting our granola and hearing the crunch as we chow down. Truly, we can be mindful in *any* moment, as long as we are paying attention.

We don't want to focus solely on paying attention, but on *how* we are paying attention. One of the qualities of mindful attention is kindness. If we are noticing what is going on and severely critiquing it, that's not mindful awareness. A whole set of practices can teach us how to be kinder and more compassionate to ourselves and the world around us. The reason we have a whole set of practices focused on this is because our brains tend to be jerks. Seriously. We are all "blessed" with something called a negativity bias, which is the tendency of the mind to seek out and focus on the difficult or negative experiences in our lives. This bias means we will likely pick apart an experience and focus on what's wrong with it rather than on what's right with it, or just simply what *is* with it.

On top of our natural tendency, companies *want* us to think there is something wrong with us so they can fix it with their clothes, makeup, video games, diet plans, and so on and so forth. Remember how we talked about companies being really focused on getting us to buy all the stuff? It is in a company's interest to fan the flames of our personal judgments and dissatisfaction. Part of their marketing is to make you think there's a problem to be solved and that they are the ones who can solve it for you. (Isn't that helpful and convenient?) Think about it: if we were really okay with ourselves and our lives, how much less would we buy? If we can fortify ourselves through mindfulness and compassion practices and develop a sense of okayness with how we are, we are less easily manipulated into buying things to make us feel better.

To be a human means to have hard things happen in our lives. To have things that feel icky. Some hard things are small, like feeling annoyed with our sibling when they bust into our rooms for the millionth time. Some hard things are huge, like losing a loved one or witnessing injustice. It is very much to our benefit to learn to be able to hang out with those feelings for a bit. To see what happens when we don't run away from them. To handle them with care. I would argue, stay with me here, that being able to sit with hard things—without running away, lashing out, or shutting completely down—is perhaps one of the most important things we as humans can learn how to do. It's scary. It is one of the most difficult things we can learn to do. And it is worth it. It is how we take a crappy experience and process and grow from it. It is how we free our bodies from the stress of that experience and move forward. It is how we figure out how to take wise action in line with our values and causing the least amount of suffering to ourselves and others. It is how we live fully.

And this is where mindfulness comes in. Our kind, gentle attention first allows us to start noticing our habits without criticizing ourselves for them. We can take the approach of, *Hmm . . . that's interesting that I do that.* We can figure out what is helping us and what is not. We can start to shift those unhealthy patterns of behaviors and thoughts toward new ones. We can remain patient with the process, knowing that we won't get it right on the first try. This last piece is extra important: We will not change overnight. It will take work. We have to want something different for ourselves to make something different happen. We have to trust that it is a process that will unfold, if we stay awake to see it through and develop the care it takes to prioritize healthy choices.

What happens when we take this lens and turn it on our everyday technology habits? Mindfulness encourages us to see what's going on without judging ourselves for it. The more lightness and good humor we can bring to our investigation, the less likely we are to get defensive. When we get defensive, we shut down. When we stay open, we can be more authentic and honest about what's going on, not just with ourselves, but also with our friends and family. If you're a newbie tech user, go in eyes wide open and see if you notice the push and pull of technology from the get-go. If you're an old hand, it's time to get curious about what's going on and see how much you can learn about yourself by taking a step back.

It Is Bigger than the "I"

We need to hit a giant pause button and offer a caveat here. Some problems related to technology use are not going to be fixed by each of us independently taking a mindful approach. Some problems with technology can and need to be addressed at the level of policy and design. I don't advocate for an individual awareness approach to technology use over a collective call to action to ask for government regulation of, and internal redesign within, these companies. I advocate for a self-focused approach alongside demands for policy change. In fact, as we start to understand not just our own experience, but our experience within the context of this larger system, it can be quite motivating to join the call for change so we don't have to work so dang hard to untangle ourselves.

The Center for Humane Technology was founded by tech insiders including Tristan Harris, who were concerned about the negative impact of tech use on our world. They're looking to create change in our system by educating the public, educating technology creators to keep ethics in mind as they design, and advocating for policy change and regulation. Through a project called #MySocialTruth, teens are invited to read and share their stories about how for-profit social media platforms have created serious challenges and suffering for users. This collective voice is more likely to create change than each of us alone. To connect with this movement for change, you could check out what others are sharing and even contribute your own story. Another option might be to watch *The Social Dilemma*, a film about how technology is designed to steal your attention, with friends and family, or you might organize a screening for your school community to talk about implications in the film. At the policy level, you might even get in touch with the lawmakers in your area to encourage them to support legislation that regulates big tech. We can care for ourselves while making our voices heard.

CHAPTER 5

Creating a Mindful Tech Diet

When you click out of Netflix after watching a whole season of a show, only to realize it's one a.m. and you have to go to school the next day, that is the perfect moment to check in with yourself. How are you feeling? Have you been mindful of the past three hours? What happened to the time?

Many aspects of technology hijack our attention so that we become disconnected from the present moment. When we're not paying attention, we can easily lose track of time and our surroundings. We might be caught up in habitual reactions rather than making time for thoughtful responses. We might communicate in ways that do not actually serve our basic human needs or those of others. We can start to have a sense of not being fully connected to our lives and the people in them. We can lose our connection to our bodies. We can lose ourselves.

Furthermore, many of us actually use technology to disconnect *on purpose*. We find whatever is happening in our lives too difficult, so we look for an escape route. People have all sorts of escape routes, and some are healthier than others. Food, running, alcohol, sleep, drugs, hanging out with friends, even meditation, can all be outs. Our phones and computers are easy portals to other worlds. That math problem is hard, but that YouTube video is easy. This awkward lull in conversation is hard, but checking my texts is easy. My disappointed feeling about my crap grade on this test is hard, but watching another episode on Netflix is easy. Truth be told, I often want to do the easy thing over the hard thing. In fact, we *all* have at least some desire to do the easy, comfortable thing. Humans have an innate drive toward comfort and ease. And there's nothing wrong with having some escape routes when things get too hard or overwhelming. But that drive toward ease may prevent us from doing the hard, messy work that it takes to turn toward what is uncomfortable.

Tech companies are intentionally manipulating us and preying on those very human tendencies and habits. So what we can do with that information? Ideally, out of all of this, we'd like to create a healthy technology diet. What does that mean, exactly?

I find the analogy of food useful when I'm thinking about what it means to use my technology in a healthy way. First and foremost, I love food, and I love to think about it. Everyone eats food, right? Some people eat more. Some people eat less. If you eat too much of any food for your body, whether it's baby carrots or cake, you will feel like crap. But you can eat until you're stuffed sometimes, and you can eat some junk food too, without totally obliterating your overall health. If you eat the right amount of nutritious food for *you*, food that fuels your body with the right balance of nutrients, then you will feel your healthiest.

We can think about our technology use this way too. One thing we know technology can do is rapidly fill our minds with content. Following the old adage "you are what you eat," it is true that whatever we put into our minds is what we'll think about. If all we do is fill our minds with first-person shooter games, that fills our psyche. Similarly, if all we do is scroll through doctored images of celebrities and our friends looking their best, that influences what we believe people (ourselves included) should look and be like. Can those activities be a part of our mental diet? Of course. Are they going to impact people differently? Definitely. We need to be aware that what we feed our minds creates our mental landscape. Questions we can ask ourselves as part of this journey: What do I put into my mind? Is what I am putting into my mind feeding the kind of psyche I want to have?

It's not just the what, however, but how much. Just as we can overfill our bodies with food, we can overfill our minds with content. Our minds *need* time to rest, digest, and decompress. If we are constantly consuming content in every spare minute of our day, there's very little opportunity for that rest and digest state. Just as our bodies need time to extract nutrition from food, so too does our mind need time to process incoming information. It can't keep up with its information filing, connecting, recall, and making new meaning without that space. Aha! moments bubble up in those spaces. Big-picture ideas can weave together in those spaces. Can you think of a time when you've had an aha! moment? It feels amazing!

Technology use has lots of nourishing aspects. We can easily connect to friends and family, seeing them through screens even when they are far away. We can learn about any topic we are interested in. We can create and share our talents, interests, and joys with others who feel similarly. If there is not a local community that supports an aspect of our identity, we can likely find it online. We can be inspired by following people who are making an impact in the world. We can relieve stress through entertainment, like watching YouTube videos. Our lives can absolutely be enhanced through technology, if we make healthy choices.

And this doesn't mean we *never* consume things that are unhealthy, or *never* consume too much. Just as I occasionally throw down a pint of Ben & Jerry's (Mint Chocolate Cookie is my favorite), I also sometimes watch Netflix for hours until two a.m. and manage to stay relatively healthy. I can engage in behavior that is not the healthiest, and as long as it's in balance with nourishing technology behaviors and other activities in my life, I feel pretty certain I'm going to be okay.

After all, it doesn't just matter what you do in front of a screen, but what you do when you're not in front of a screen. According to the Mindsight Institute, our minds need a balance of the following activities for us to feel well: sleep, social engagement and face-to-face interactions, movement, downtime, self-reflection, playtime, and work time or focused attention. So start asking yourself: Do I incorporate all these elements into my day? Do I take care of my mind by leaving time for off-screen activities and by choosing nourishing on-screen activities?

How do we get to a place where we feel like we have a healthy technology diet and we make space for all the mind-care activities?

Mindful Reflection

Let's start by getting clear about your own aspirations for your life and how your technology use aligns with that. Using the journal prompts throughout the book, along with the tracking exercises and quizzes in this chapter, you can personalize this book to fit your own needs and your own life.

As you go through these, see how honest you can be. Sometimes, you might come across a question and realize your answer is, *I have no idea!* That's awesome. You've just found an area to consider. Sometimes you'll come across an answer and be like, *Whoa, that's embarrassing.* See if you can cut yourself some slack. We're all trying to figure this out together. If you find yourself feeling defensive, saying, "Yeah, but I *need* my phone on at school because my mom says I have to, and she gets mad if I don't and that's not my fault and . . ." you can relax. No one here is criticizing you. Come back to the intention: we are looking at habits that serve us and those that don't.

Regardless of your answers, the point is absolutely not that you are better or worse based on how you use technology. We are used to all sorts of shaming that comes along with examining our habits. And then we feel bad. And then we get defensive. Instead, see if you can celebrate finding areas where you have an opportunity to make some new choices! You've done it. You've gained awareness. Internal high five.

If you haven't gone through the big-picture journal prompts yet, you can find them on pages 25, 51, 65, 133, and 152. These are great ways to gain clarity for yourself and also have conversations with parents, teachers, and friends about how technology functions in your life. If you have already done these, you can go straight to the values assessment. Either way, grab your journal, a pen and paper, or even a Google Doc if that's going to make it happen, and get reflecting.

Values: What Really Matters to You?

A value is a standard of behavior or judgment about how one should live one's life. We all have a set of values, whether or not we realize it, that can impact the choices we make. Getting clear on those values can help us see whether the choices we are making support them. If you dig down deep, what's really important to you? Like, if you were an elder sitting in a rocking chair at your nursing home, what would you want to have seen or demonstrated as part of your life?

Choose from the list below the five values that are most important to you. You may also want to investigate qualities not on this list. Feel free to add your own!

acceptance	beauty
adaptability	bravery
adventure	calmness
ambition	challenge
amusement	cheerfulness
artistry	cleanliness
authenticity	compassion
balance	confidence

cooperation
creativity
diversity
entertainment
equity
excellence
excitement
flexibility
friendliness
generosity
gratefulness
helpfulness
honesty
inclusion
independence
innovation
intelligence
justice
leadership
love
loyalty
openness

optimism
order and organization
peacefulness
perseverance
playfulness
popularity
realism
reason and logic
security
self-control
sensitivity
simplicity
spirituality
strength
success
teamwork
truth
warmth
wisdom
wonder
Insert your ideas here:

Next, take each of the values you identified and do a freewrite on what they mean to you. For example, if authenticity was a value you chose, what do you mean by that? What does that look like and feel like in your life? What examples demonstrate that value? Who do you know that shows that value? Go through each one and get clear on what you'd like to be guiding your choices. These are not set in stone, nor do they discount other values.

Choose one of those values and think about a time when you really lived it. What did that feel like in your body? What kinds of thoughts did you have?

In what ways do you live your values while using technology? In what ways does your technology use not align with your values?

What changes, if any, would you make to really support living your values? (Think about what you might want to do *more* of and what you might want to do *less* of.)

Charting Your Use

How much we *think* we use our technology and how much we *actually* use our technology are two entirely different beasts. (This applies to how much time we spend doing other things too.) I learned this when I checked out my screen-time tracker on my phone. *But seriously, how did those numbers get so high without me realizing it?*

You could investigate this in a few different ways.

1. For one day, track your use manually on a chart or a list and then add up the major categories. See page 99 for a sample chart.
2. Use the "Screen Time" feature on iPhones. You might have to dig in a little (it counts GPS use, for example, which I'm not as curious about), but it will provide the data. Other screen-use tracking apps include Freedom, Moment, and Social Fever.
3. On your computer, use trackers like TimeCamp or Toggl to keep track of all that you do (keeping in mind that these "free" programs are likely recording all your activities for their data collection).

However you choose to go about it, take note of the total amount of time you spend on your screen (or screens, if you want to include computers, tablets, and game consoles). Then break that time down into categories.

As you complete this tracking exercise, it may also be helpful to journal about anything that your time tracker doesn't capture. As we

		Monday	Tuesday	Wednesday	Thursday	Friday	Saturday	Sunday
	Total Time							
Top Time Sinks	Example: email							
	Example: social media							

note how we spend our time, we might also gain insight into how we feel as we are using screens or any habits we have (such as quickly checking texts or popping over to YouTube while in the middle of homework). Don't overthink this. Just notice if anything stands out to you as you bring more awareness to your tech use.

Finally, take a moment to check out your chart. Did anything surprise you? Did anything concern you? Is there anything you would like to spend more or less time doing? Check it against your values: Do your online activities align with those values? Are they getting you where you want to be in life, and are you spending your time the way you want?

Assessing Your Tech Use

Surveys can help us determine how and when we are using our screens. But remember, these are not meant as a value judgment. They are meant to bring awareness to different habits. You are not "bad" or "good" if you do or don't do any of these things.

It might be useful to monitor your reactions as you go through the following questions. Do you feel defensive? Proud? Embarrassed? Annoyed? This is all information that can teach us about ourselves. I remember when I first started asking myself these questions, I immediately wanted to explain away why I was spending so many meals in front of my screen. I felt defensive and annoyed. But by taking a few breaths, I could see that my defensiveness was in part because I felt embarrassed that my actions weren't aligning with my value of being present. Once I gave the defensiveness some space, I could see that if I wanted to live my values, I needed to start putting my phone and computer away while I chowed down. It helped me shift toward a behavior more in line with how I wanted to live. Don't be afraid to let your reactions have some breathing room. Keep in mind that the questions that elicit strong reactions are probably the ones you should investigate further. If you didn't care, you wouldn't have a reaction at all.

As you take the survey on the opposite page, answer the questions as honestly as you can. You may choose to make a photocopy and answer right on the survey or keep track of your answers in your journal to figure out your score at the end. I often hear questions like, *What if I'm in between? Can I choose that?* Sure! Again, this is just to raise awareness, so ultimately the questions are just guiding that awareness to particular tech habits.

So, we've spent some time looking at our values and our current tech behaviors. We may have noticed some of the ways our tech use is serving us or some of the ways it isn't. Now we can start to get more curious about our technology use *as* it is happening. Can we really see the impact? How would we go about doing that?

Insert mindfulness here.

Technology Use Survey

Choose the most accurate answer to each question and add up the points below your answers to find your total score.

How soon after waking do you usually start using technology?

More than 1 hour	30 minutes	Immediately
0	1	2

How soon before sleep do you usually stop using technology?

2 hours	1 hour	Just before sleep
0	1	2

Do you stay up later than you'd like while using technology?

Never	Sometimes	Often
0	1	2

How many meals a day do you spend in front of technology?

None	One	Two or more
0	1	2

Do you use technology to self-soothe when you're feeling upset, sad, or angry?

Never	Sometimes	Often
0	1	2

Do you use technology when you're bored?

Never	Sometimes	Often
0	1	2

Do you lose track of time on your device and spend longer than you intended?

Never	Sometimes	Often
0	1	2

Do you crave using your technology when you're not using it?

Never	Sometimes	Often
0	1	2

How many hours a day, not school-related, do you spend in front of a device?

None	One	Two or more
0	1	2

If you have a phone, do you keep it on and out at work or school?

Never	Sometimes	Always
0	1	2

How often do you get in arguments with family or friends because of your tech use?

Never	Sometimes	Often
0	1	2

Do you have your phone out or use other unrelated tabs on your computer while doing your homework?

Never	Sometimes	Always
0	1	2

How often do you notice you feel bad about yourself after scrolling through social media?

Never	Sometimes	Always
0	1	2

Do you say things online that you wouldn't say in person?

Never	Sometimes	Often
0	1	2

Do you ever notice yourself wanting more likes, comments, or feedback on your social media than you receive?

Never	Sometimes	Always
0	1	2

Do you prefer to have hard conversations over text message or through the internet rather than face-to-face?

Never	Sometimes	Always
0	1	2

Do you have limited downtime because you pick up your phone every spare moment?

Never	Sometimes	Always
0	1	2

Do you ever avoid dealing with difficult emotions or having difficult conversations by using tech?

Never	Sometimes	Always
0	1	2

Total: _____

POSSIBLE SCORE RANGE: 0–36

The higher your total score, the more likely it is that technology is having an impact on your life. If you didn't know the answer to a question, that is an area to investigate in the coming week. The whole point is to start paying attention!

It can also help to go back to the questions that had higher numbers or that you had a reaction to. Celebrate the opportunity to bring attention to that part of your life. Consider having a conversation with someone about these insights or journaling about the areas of awareness you discovered through completing this survey.

Mindfulness and Technology Use Habits

A tech behavior can easily turn into a habit, which my dictionary defines as "an acquired mode of behavior that has become nearly or completely involuntary." We do habits without thinking. We don't consider how they make us feel, if they are really how we want to be spending our time, or if they align with our values. Some habits are useful, such as brushing our teeth or showering. Some habits are less useful, such as smoking or mindlessly scrolling through social media during any free moment.

In terms of how we experience habits, they can be relatively neutral—meaning something you do mindlessly but there aren't necessarily strong cravings around it—or addictive, meaning the cravings are so strong that you continue to do something even though it may be bad for you.

Let's nerd out on this for a minute.

HOW CELLS COMMUNICATE

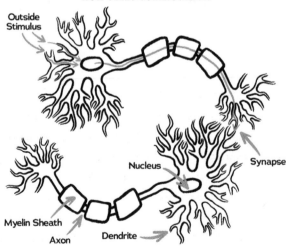

Our brains have a bunch of cells in them called neurons. Neurons pass messages among themselves, across synapses, using neurochemicals. They shoot those messages out of their axons and collect them with their dendrites. With a repeated behavior or thought (a habit), the axons are myelinated, meaning a sheath forms around the axon, and the messages can travel faster and faster. We barely even notice some of the habits we've formed, because the neurons just take such good care of us and make sure it happens.

Now, imagine we want to do something new. Say I don't want to play Snake on my phone every time I feel even an inkling of boredom. The good news is that our brains can rewire through a process called neuroplasticity. Once we start noticing our impulse to reach for the phone, we can pause. What's tricky is that the urge is going to be strong because our neurons are all myelinated up and are like, "Hey, this is what we do next! *Let's go!*" Instead, we must consciously choose, for example, to take a breath in response to that urge. In making that new choice, we start down a new neural pathway. Over time (and, if this is a deep habit, this can really take time and repeated new choices), we can begin the process of unlinking.

Boredom ➡ play Snake

and rewire:

Boredom ➡ pause and take a breath

With that change in behavior, that new pathway starts to form, the neurons get myelinated, and we are on our way!

Science of Mindfulness and Habits

Mindfulness can be useful as a habit breaker. How does mindfulness support breaking habits, even addictive ones? Well, if habits are mindless behaviors we don't even notice, practicing mindfulness makes us more likely to slow down and take moments of pause to notice impulses instead of just reacting. Because our impulses and urges are often unconscious and quick, learning how to pay attention to the sensations in the body and thoughts in the mind can help us notice the stimulus to the reaction before we do anything. In a classic sci-fi movie called *The Matrix*, the lead character famously dodges bullets because he is able to focus so completely that it seems as if time has slowed. With mindfulness, we can see the mental "bullet" coming and make a choice rather than just being hit by the impulse and reaction.

When we practice mindfulness, we start to see our thoughts as just thoughts. We don't have to act on them. And through the practice, we learn how to tolerate discomfort: *I can be uncomfortable and sit with hard feelings! I don't need my phone to make this boredom go away.* Finally, many of our habitual behaviors stem from a sense of unease. Feel bad, then react to make yourself feel better. If we are regularly practicing mindfulness and feeling better in general—happier with ourselves, more grateful, more at ease—then the urge to change that state won't be as strong. Our baseline is more chill.

While using mindfulness as an approach to supporting healthy tech habits is relatively new, strong research demonstrates how mindfulness can be used to break other habits. Judson Brewer, addiction expert, researcher, and author of *The Craving Mind: From Cigarettes to Smartphones to Love—Why We Get Hooked and How We Can Break Bad Habits*, found that a mindfulness program was twice as effective as a gold standard treatment program (those are the best!) in helping people to quit smoking. Another colleague in the field, Jean Kristeller, found mindfulness to be an effective treatment option to help people who were struggling with binge eating.

The application of mindfulness to technology use is still new, but some people are already finding tremendous benefit. In a 2016 study, researchers Manuel Gámez-Guadix and Esther Calvete found that teens who self-reported greater mindful awareness preferred in-person interactions, didn't use the internet to feel better as frequently, and didn't have as many problems related to their internet use as other teens.

Even those who identify as being addicted to technology have used mindfulness to investigate their behavior.

Former gamer and founder of Game Quitters, Cam Adair, said:

The biggest thing that helped with the cravings was becoming aware of them and disassociating with them. Meditation and exercise helped me a lot, but the biggest thing that helped with the cravings was becoming aware of them. I started to feel the sensation in my body and recognize that it was controlling me. The more I craved it and didn't feed the craving validated that I shouldn't be gaming.

While this may be an extreme example, all of us have technology habits we can explore. All of us can benefit from cultivating kindness toward ourselves and our investigation. All of us can use support in doing this, knowing we are not alone. If you do feel like your technology use is extreme and having an intensely negative impact on your life, you might explore resources on reSTART (see sidebar on page 71), look into Adair's website gamequitters.com, or even just talk to your parents about finding a local therapist who specializes in internet and gaming disorders. If it feels less urgent than that, begin your investigation into your own habits and consider discussing what you notice with friends or family.

At the end of the day, it's up to you to decide what works for you and what doesn't. Consider this a giant science experiment on yourself. What can you learn? What happens when you *really* start paying attention? Are there subtle shifts you can make to feel more alive in your life? More connected? Better rested? Less distracted? Less stressed?

As my mindfulness teachers often say, don't believe me. Don't believe a single word I say. But do try it out. Do be honest with yourself. Do see what happens.

Let's get started. What follows are some general ways of being when using technology. These are value driven and recommended to make us more aware and compassionate while using our devices. We can hold them in our minds and check our choices and behaviors against them. This section is not meant to be exhaustive, and you get to decide what might serve you best. It is also not meant to say we are always mindful or always feel the same way. This is just the general direction we may try to head if we want a healthier relationship with tech.

Guidelines for Mindful Tech Use

To be mindful of our technology use means we are:

- Grateful for the opportunity to have technology in our lives.
- Fully aware of our own habits of use, without lying to ourselves or others about it.
- Clear about how our habits of use impact all parts of us: our minds, bodies, and social relationships.
- Clear about how our technology use relates to our bigger goals and aspirations in life.
- Clear about what we intend to do before we get on our technology and how long we want to be on it.
- Connected with our minds and bodies while using technology to observe the impact.
- Free from impulsively distracting ourselves from any uncomfortable emotions or thoughts.
- Free from needing a particular response from people on social platforms.
- Honest, kind, and compassionate with our communication on social platforms.
- Kind and compassionate with our inner narrator while engaging with technology.
- Forgiving of ourselves when we are not mindful or make mistakes.

5 Mindfulness Practices to Use While on Technology

How do we keep mindfulness guidelines alive? What do we actually do? While you're engaged with technology, a few general practices will help you stay alert and aware of what's going on. Try one of these techniques the next time you're about to get started with your tech and see how the experience feels.

Scan to listen.

1. Slow your roll. Before you start any tech session, take a moment to set an intention for what you want to do while you're on there. Are you trying to do serious, focused work to pound out that essay due tomorrow? Are you looking to zone out by watching your favorite YouTube influencer crash and burn at the skate park? If you have a series of tasks, you might even consider writing them down with a time stamp approximating how long you think each task will take you. It can be a first step toward not being sucked down the black hole of baby animal videos or conspiracy theory Reddit threads.

So, check yourself before you wreck yourself:

- Why are you getting on your device?
- What are you hoping to do while you're there?
- How much time would you like to spend?

2. Hit the pause button. As you're using your devices, consider setting a timer at regular intervals to pause and see what you need. If it's a longer task, like writing a research paper, you may set it for regular twenty-minute intervals. If it's a series of shorter tasks, you might set the timer for how long you think each part should take. When the timer goes off, pause and check in. *How do I feel right now? What do I need right now? Can I keep at it? Should I keep at it? Am I intending to write this essay but actually reading BuzzFeed? How does my body feel? Should I get up and walk around?* Giving ourselves this moment to check in can help us make a choice for the next moment, rather than just impulsively following some urge to check text messages and

Screen Fatigue?

Feeling lethargic and brain-dead after a long period staring at your screen? Try these exercises to help perk you up!

- Close your eyes and relax the muscles around those eyes.
- Look as far away from the screen as you can (out a window, if one is available).
- Take three breaths, focusing on a strong inhale.
- Drop your shoulders down away from your ears.
- Slowly drop your left ear to your left shoulder. Roll your chin to your chest. Lift your right ear to your right shoulder. Continue back and forth.
- Side bend to the left and then to the right with your arms overhead. Then straighten and drop your arms to your sides. Gently twist your upper body to one side and then the other to stretch the spine.
- Stand up! Go for a walk! Save yourself!

then being lost an hour later, wondering where the time went (and why the dang essay didn't write itself in the meantime).

3. Locate yourself in space. Oftentimes we get swept up in our experience of tech and lose track of our physical space. Tuning in to the world around you and your internal sensations will give you a way to return after you've been tossed about.

Start by having a sense of the physical space around you.

Really notice the height of the ceiling above you, the distance to the floor below.

Turn all the way around and check out the space behind you.

Notice the distance in front of you to the wall or window.

Now, have a sense of your body in that space.

Feel your feet on the ground.

Backs of the legs connected.

Butt pressing into whatever you are sitting on.

Can you expand your awareness to then have a sense of your whole body sitting?

Feel the outline of the body, the position, the warmth or coolness. Really feel into being here.

Now, what does it physically feel like to make contact with your phone (or computer or console)? Notice the texture of the device. How does it feel to tap the phone, press down on the keys, or move the controller around?

As you get settled into your tech use—whether that means starting your homework, gaming, or scrolling through social media—can you keep part of your mind anchored on the body? When your attention becomes engulfed, can you come back to your body and physical space around you to check in from time to time? Can you come back to feeling the device in your hands or under your fingers?

4. Check your internal weather. When you are pausing, or ready to step away from your device for a moment, try this out. Our internal weather is really important in deciding what to do next. If you are feeling dull and sluggish while doing homework, it might be time to get up and move around. Even if that means you are taking time away and might seem unproductive, you will likely gain that time back through being more efficient in your work when you return. If you are scrolling through social media and notice you feel angry about a comment some troll made, that might also be a good time to check in with the body and take a break before you say something you wish you hadn't. Maybe you wait until the rage passes and come up with an articulate response. Either way, make space to act from a place of clarity and wisdom.

Close your eyes and reconnect to the body.

Feel the touch points of your body making contact with the floor or chair or whatever is underneath you.

Now, notice how your body feels. (Heavy? Light? Loose? Tight? Jittery?)

Notice the state of your mind. (Racing? Settled? Sluggish? Alert?)

Notice what emotions are present. (Happiness? Uneasiness? Fear? Frustration? Jealousy? Excitement?)

In general, what's your sense of how you are feeling in this moment?

Knowing that, ask yourself, what is my next step?

5. Center the good. It can be easy to take our technology for granted or even hate on it. But how often do we really take the time to appreciate the many ways it helps us live our best life? Already, midmorning at the time of writing, I bought a few presents for family, checked my calendar to figure out what the heck I am supposed to do today, and started working on this book without fear that I might spill my coffee on my pages and lose it forever. (Can you imagine what it must have been like to write everything out longhand before computers?! I mean, I guess the upside was that you could say your dog ate your homework and it was a plausible excuse.)

What might it be like to pause after a session on your technology and consider the ways your life is better for having this tool? How would it feel to truly let those ideas sink into your body. *Wow . . . this is such a gift.* Let's give it a go.

Take a moment to let your eyes close. Reflect on your time with your technology.

What was easier, better, or more joyful because you had this device?

Did you get to connect with people who are important to you? Did you get to quickly look up information about something you knew nothing about? Did you get to create something beautiful? Did you have some tool to organize all your tasks so you could complete them more easily?

What need did technology meet for you? A sense of connection? Knowledge? Efficiency? Organization?

Notice what it feels like in your body to have a need met. Warm? Settling? Energizing? Light?

Give thanks to the many people who made this moment possible—those who invented and designed these devices, those who manufactured them, those who packaged and shipped them to you, and those who delivered them. Thank you.

When you are ready, open your eyes. Notice if practicing this exercise has allowed you to experience your device in a new way.

We know mindfulness can help us really wake up as we use our technology. It is a way of orienting toward our own experiences, seeing our habits, and regaining agency in an area that can feel uncontrollable. It invites us back to our real-time, present-moment experience. Once we've regained the awareness that is so easily lost while on technology, we are no longer at the mercy of our habits and the tech companies that prey on them. We get to choose.

The Environmental Impact of Our Tech

There are some pretty big questions we don't often stop to ask.

Like, where do our tablets, smartphones, desktops, laptops, and game consoles come from?

The box? The phone store?

Le sigh. It's not good, y'all. Our tech is made up of different kinds of metals that must be extracted from the earth: iron, aluminum, magnesium, copper, silver, gold, graphite, and lithium, to name just a few. That mining destroys the ecosystem of the mined area and the area around the mining area, not to mention the communities living in those areas. It also requires tremendous amounts of energy to dig up and transport these metals, which releases tremendous amounts of greenhouse gas emissions into the atmosphere.

And then we dump our precious phones into a landfill two years later to get the newest model. (While we'd like to think we recycle them, overall, we don't.) There's an endless market for the newest, fastest, shiniest phone, so there's an endless need for new precious metals, mining, and environmental destruction. (Side note: this is called *planned obsolescence*, in which companies intentionally make things to be quickly thrown away rather than fixed and used for a long time.)

Also, where are all my photos actually stored?

Errrr . . . up in the sky?

Our uploaded photos live in data centers (warehouses full of servers), along with our tweets, YouTube videos, Google Docs, and anything else in the cloud. These data centers require, yet again, a tremendous amount of energy to run. And much of that energy is produced by burning fossil fuels.

What do we do?

It's really easy to not think about where our technology actually comes from. And you know that squirmy uncomfortable feeling that comes from knowing? That's good! It's your conscience saying that it doesn't want you to destroy your planet. It wants you to make a choice at a personal, and possibly societal, level that protects where we live. Don't be afraid to hear it.

After all, if we stopped and thought about it, we might think twice about immediately getting the best, fastest, prettiest, and newest gadget. On an individual level, you can recycle most electronics (please do!) and wait a little longer before buying new items. Some small start-up companies are trying to do things better, like Fairphone in the Netherlands, which is working on better sourcing, replaceable parts, and longevity of their smartphones. If you really want to see impactful change, lending your voice to a collective movement is the way to go. In 2018, Greenpeace used civil disobedience and crowd support to encourage Samsung to move to 100 percent renewable energy sources and accountability around their supply chain. In response, Samsung made a commitment to work toward those goals. Greenpeace is also calling out Amazon for not living up to their commitment to get their data centers running on 100 percent renewables, with more transparency around energy consumption. If you want to be involved with this work, consider signing up to be part of an environmental group's volunteer corps. Part of our duty as mindful consumers is to minimize the damage caused by our buying habits.

CHAPTER 6

Attention Hijacks and Mindful Approaches

This is the choose-your-own-adventure portion of the book. What follows is a list of real attention hijacks that affect people, followed by a way to approach each problem mindfully. Based on some of the personal struggles you may have uncovered in chapter 5, find the headings in this chapter that seem appropriate and read more about the specific approaches that may serve you. Remember, there's no shame here. This is about learning, experimenting, and ultimately making your own choice about what works for you.

If you are a new tech user who has yet to encounter these obstacles, this is a great place to learn from those who have come before you so you can sidestep some of these struggles. Read through and set yourself up for success by creating structures to help you navigate the hijacks that might arise as you start to use your phone or computer more frequently. As I've said before, you are in an easier position to create healthy habits because you haven't created all those tech-habit grooves in your brain yet.

Remember, when you are experimenting, the changes you make don't have to last *forever*. You may commit to small changes just to see how they make you feel. But changing something for a day or even a week may not really give you a sense of how it could feel over time. And some changes will take time to reset to a new normal. So, tell yourself it's not forever, and give it time. Then get really curious. What happens? How are you being affected? What is different or the same? This awareness can help us resist urges to turn back toward that which does not serve us.

👁 Hijack 1: Sleep Deprivation

I'm not tired, you're tired! Okay, we're all tired. The number-one concern I hear from my students is that they are not getting enough sleep, often because they stay on technology late into the night. As we get tired, our willpower and defenses are down, and we are much more susceptible to attention hijacking than we might be earlier in the day. One more episode? Why not? Try to level up? Count me in. Respond to that snarky text message? Definitely.

This is on top of the fact that the circadian rhythm of teens runs later into the evening and morning than that of adults, so it's already harder for you to get to sleep earlier. Your melatonin, which is triggered in response to darkness and helps cue your body into a sleepy state, releases later in the night. It turns out that young people, more than adults, are extra susceptible to light exposure. If you are bathing in the blue light of your device, your body doesn't realize it's time to hit the hay and will suppress the melatonin release. Even being on technology excessively throughout the day can make it harder to go to sleep and stay asleep at night. In addition to blue light interrupting our natural rhythms, technology tends to rev up our nervous system with engaging content and interactions. This makes it even tougher to wind down when it's time to get some shut-eye.

So what do we do?

Mindful Approach 1: Create Personal Boundaries

Start paying attention to how you feel physically while scrolling, gaming, or watching videos late into the evening. What does it feel like to play *Call of Duty* at one a.m.? Is your body buzzing and your heart racing? Conversely, do you feel heavy with sleep but resist the pull? Are you allowing YouTube to autoplay the next suggestion and the next, even as your eyes get heavy? Do you check your phone in the middle of the night when you get up to use the bathroom? How do you feel the next morning after a night or two of staying up too late scrolling or playing?

With mindfulness, we always start with noticing. When we tune into our body, we start to really be aware of how crappy it feels to miss out on a lot of sleep. Then we offer a compassionate response. *Hey, Self, I hear it doesn't feel so good to be on the computer or phone until all hours of the night. Let's experiment with some boundaries.*

What might those healthy boundaries look like for you? Here are some ways of protecting your sleep space:

- **Eight p.m., screens off.** Choose a time, ahead of time, to get off your phone. Set your alarm for that time to remind you. Tell other people about your time, and invite them to remind you (gently, of course) that you've set that limit for yourself. Doctors generally recommend that you stop using technology an hour or two before bed to help with the blue light effect.

- **Get an alarm clock.** That way, you don't have to have your phone next to your bed. In fact, I would really recommend putting your charging station anywhere but your bedroom. Okay, and the bathroom, because that's gross.

- **Create a soothing bedtime routine.** If we are totally in the habit of looking at our phones right before bed, and then we stop doing that . . . then *what do we do?* When I first banned my phone from my bedtime routine, the embarrassing truth is, I seriously didn't know the answer.

Here are a few possibilities that you might build your healthy bedtime routine around:

- *Read.* A book. A paper book. It's so satisfying to get lost in someone else's drama. But I will say, relearning to love reading can be hard if your brain hasn't been practicing, so start light and give yourself time to rebuild stamina.
- *Draw or doodle.* I know there are a bunch of creative folks out there. Keep a sketchbook next to your bed and create! And for you not-so-artistic bunch, coloring books aren't just for kids. Grab some colored pencils or crayons and a coloring book and get going.
- *Use your phone (on airplane mode) to take advantage of the incredible array of mindfulness apps.* I find body scans and yoga nidra particularly helpful right at bedtime, but you can explore and find out what works best for you. You really need to know thyself on this one. Can you actually keep your phone on airplane mode, or will this be a slippery slope?
- *Listen to music.* Maybe not heavy metal, but something low-key and soothing.
- *Keep a gratitude journal.* Take a moment at the end of each day to remember the good moments of the day. The more we take time to recognize what we appreciate in life, the more we tend to enjoy our lives.
- *Drink a cup of tea.* Chamomile with honey or lemon is particularly soothing.
- *Insert your idea(s) here.*

Hijack 2: Morning Phone

Your phone alarm goes off, you roll over to stop it, and through your blurry, groggy eyes you see that you have five new Snaps, twenty new Instagram notifications, and four text messages. Your curiosity about what these all say gives you a little jolt of adrenaline, and you find yourself scrolling and responding before you have even gotten up to pee. And you really have to pee.

The way you start your morning can really influence how the rest of your day unfolds. If, within the first five minutes of waking up, you've already had twenty social interactions and skimmed through three Reddit threads, that's a lot of content to carry forth. Our minds are prone to obsessing over anything unnerving and can easily start spinning. Not only is this unpleasant in the moment, but it can also distract us from getting ourselves ready for the day, and it can set a tone for the morning that is hard to recover from.

Mindful Approach 2: Morning Care Routines

We can try a number of strategies to give ourselves space in the morning.

It is really helpful to have an **alarm clock** that is not your phone. You can't help but see notifications if your phone is your alarm. It's too easy. (Not to mention that notification buzzes or dings can interrupt your sleep.) If you insist on keeping your phone as your alarm clock, at the very least put it on airplane mode overnight.

Set up a **morning routine** that feels nourishing to you. Maybe you'll challenge yourself: how much can you do *before* turning on your phone? Spend the extra five minutes you might be scrolling just enjoying the coziness of still being in bed, not having to move yet. Consider trying a simple yoga posture such as child's pose, or even some easy stretches. Brush your teeth, take a shower, get dressed. Give yourself the time and space to just exist without having to answer to anyone.

Consider trying a **brief meditation**. Page 87 also has some great suggestions for meditation apps that teens have found helpful. Inviting yourself to center, focus, and ground before moving into your day can make it feel easier.

One thing that amazes me when I leave space in the morning is the way my life seems to organize itself more easily. I am clearer on

Morning Meditation

Scan to listen.

From whatever position you find your body—lying down, sitting up, standing—take a moment to lengthen the spine. Deepen your breath down into the belly.

Bring your attention to the parts of your body making contact with your bed, a chair, or the floor. Sense your connection through these objects to the ground.

Find an easy anchor for your attention. You could continue to focus on that connection of the body with the ground, or you could shift to focusing on your breath moving in and out. (Spend a minute or two here.)

Consider whether there's a word or phrase that might help you move into the day more easily. It could be something like focus, patience, or strength. Call that word to mind and notice how it feels in the body to hold that thought.

Now, as you start to bring slow movement into the body, try to move with the quality of the word you chose.

the things I need to get done and when they need to happen. I am also clearer on the things that *do not* have to get done immediately, and I can prioritize more effectively.

Be selective with what you take in in the morning. If you know a particular website or game creates stress in your body, consider saving it for after school or later in the afternoon. Start the day in a chill space.

👁️ Hijack 3: Time Sink

The digital content we have access to is extremely compelling, and it is all too easy to lose minutes, hours, and days of our lives to meaningless, unfulfilling activities. As we learned earlier, apps and websites are intentionally designed to suck us out of our present reality and into a virtual world where we have little sense of how much time has passed, because the Netflix series rolls on, the Instagram feed never ends, and the TikTok stream runs *forever*.

👍 Mindful Approach 3: Time Check

Check yourself. How do you approach your time? If we think of our time as precious—a finite resource—does that change how we use it? Sometimes just reminding ourselves that we have a choice can help break the spell of momentum.

If we aren't down for losing so much time, what can we do to keep one foot in this world so we don't end up in the virtual world longer than we intend? One easy hack is to set a timer for the amount of time you'd like to spend using tech. This gives a sense of how long (*Wait, it's been half an hour?*) or how short (*Wait, I've only been working on this paper for five minutes? It feels like it's been five hours!*) you've been on. When the timer goes off, you can reevaluate if you'd like to continue on the current track, reset the timer for another set length of time, or maybe take a break.

Another way to limit our time is to use the time-limiting features on our devices. You can decide how long you feel okay about being on different apps (for example, I don't limit my time on my meditation app, but I do limit Instagram), and you can choose which times of day you feel okay about being on the screen.

Ophthalmologists (eye docs) suggest that every twenty minutes, we take a break from staring at screens to give our eyes and bodies a break from whatever hunched, strained position we've assumed during that time. If we move a little, we help blood circulate through our system, which actually helps our brains work better. Once our brains are back online, we can make a conscious choice about whether we'd like to come back to whatever we were doing or do something else.

Body Breaks

Scan to listen.

EYE STRETCHES

- Warm your hands by rubbing them together. Then press your palms gently over your eyes.
- Lift your gaze and visually scan a space. Even better, look out a window for a few minutes and let your eyes scan objects far away.
- Close your eyes. Take three slow breaths before opening them.

BODY STRETCHES

- Shoulder opener: Clasp your hands at your low back and roll your shoulders backward to open up your chest.
- Side bends: Reach your arms up overhead and bend to one side, then the other.
- Chair twists: Sitting in a chair, sit up nice and tall and twist to one side and then the other.
- Leg swings: Stand on one leg and swing the opposite leg back and forth for ten to twenty seconds. Repeat, standing on the other leg.

Hijack 4: Time Fill

You are waiting for the bus (or in line at the grocery store. Or waiting for your friend to come pick you up. Or walking in the hallway between classes. Or on the pooper) when you feel that familiar itch. Your hand automatically reaches for your phone every moment that something else isn't demanding your attention. You aren't looking for any particular message or information. It's just an impulse at this point. And something will always be there to capture your attention.

We don't give ourselves downtime because we don't have to. There's always something to fill that space. We have this habit of occupying the mind every waking moment. (Or even sleeping moments, if you keep your television running and phone turned on all night long.) The more we are in the habit of filling that space, the more we will continue to fill it. Remember habits and myelination of the neurons? It's part of the human condition that it's hard to be alone with our thoughts (people have chosen to shock themselves rather than be left alone with nothing to do for fifteen minutes). But just because it's hard doesn't mean we shouldn't do it.

Mindful Approach 4: Schedule Boredom

Our brains need downtime between stimuli. They need time to process. To integrate. And if we are constantly shoving new stuff in there, that interferes with our ability to build meaningful connections between experiences and information. Think about it. If we were constantly eating, our stomachs wouldn't have time to digest the last bit of food we swallowed. Our digestive system needs periods of rest, just as our brains need downtime to process and recover. Taking time to let your mind rest on something with low stimulation, such as gazing out the window or at your hands, gives your brain space to do some background processing without added interference.

Also, some flavors of boredom are really good for you. It turns out that people do more creative and interesting problem-solving when they've been forced into a mundane, boring task ahead of time. This is because the mind gets restless and starts looking for ways to entertain itself, so it gets more innovative as it pulls at different ideas from its recesses. I still remember the way my kid mind would wander during epic daylong drives to my grandmother's house and the delightfully satisfying aha! moments I found myself having.

So let's get bored! Set an intention to replace a time when you usually reach for your phone out of boredom with a plan to sit with yourself, phone free. Maybe that's right when you get picked up from school. Or as you walk home. Maybe it's when you are in the bathroom. (Let's be real. Being on your phone on the toilet is gross anyway.) Put a tiny wedge between moments of your day. Let your eyes rest on a plant, or even close them. If you are outside, feel the sunshine or wind on your skin. Invite your whole being to sink into that very moment and soak it up. Maybe that scheduled block will lead to your next eureka moment! Or maybe it will just be a mini brain break of no consequence. Either way, after the initial discomfort that can accompany slowing down, see what else you can find in that space. A little moment of ease? A pocket of joy? A moment of rest?

👁 Hijack 5: The Need to Multitask

> My tolerance for doing one thing at a time or doing something with no entertainment is pretty much nonexistent. I generally have to be doing a couple things at a time or be on my phone to feel fully entertained.
>
> —Elsie, eighth grader

Our minds crave stimulation. They love it. They feed off it. But they are also fatigued and overwhelmed by it. We already went over the myth of multitasking on page 68. So, we know that it doesn't work for us. We know we can't be as accurate, as deep in our thinking, or as efficient if we are multitasking. And yet, we want to so badly!

👍 Mindful Approach 5: Single Task

Okay, this one might be hard at first! Many of us have gotten out of the habit of giving our full attention to just one thing. But do it. Do one thing. For a week (A day? An hour? You choose an amount of time you think you can handle.), experiment with just focusing on the one thing in front of you. Practice giving your full attention to the one thing. Hype it up! Make it as fun as you can. Pretend it's the most interesting thing you've ever done. You can't even believe that you can experience that thing! We do have some power to direct our thoughts, so try experimenting with what it's like to intentionally change your attitude toward a task. If that feels fake, you can at least notice the resistance and try relaxing your body and reassuring yourself with your mind: *I am not super interested in this, but I know I can do it. And then it will be over. And I'll probably have done it better for just setting up the time to make it happen.* Whatever you can muster up to encourage yourself can be helpful.

Try out your single tasking with something less painful for you to focus on. For example, what does it feel like to turn on your favorite music and just listen? No videos. No conversations. Fully listen. Can you immerse yourself in the song? Notice the rise and fall of the melody. Can you pick out the different lines of instrumentation, then simply return to the song as a whole? Notice how your body responds as the song crescendos and decrescendos. Can you listen to the song all the way through?

Or try "savor eating," the mindful approach listed after this one.

Then graduate to harder experiences. Maybe it's keeping your phone put away for a car ride with your mom and fully listening to a conversation with her. (How would you listen if she were about to go on a month-long work trip?) Maybe it's those chapters you have to read for language arts. (How would you read it if it held information that was important to you?) Whatever it is, what is it like to approach it as though it is totally fascinating? But, like, really try on this approach and believe in it.

👁 Hijack 6: Distracted Eating

Truth? This is one of the hardest habits for me to break. It is so easy for me to bring my phone to the table and scroll through Instagram while I nosh on a bowl of cereal, or to work my way through email as I chow down on lunch. But I am aware that I am missing out when I do this, and it is an area where I keep trying to make better choices.

Why?

A few reasons.

1. **I don't really enjoy my food when I'm distracted.** And I like food, dang it! I want to be there to enjoy it. Whenever I am scrolling through Instagram, writing emails, or reading the news, I totally miss whatever delicious food was in front of me. That oatmeal with maple syrup? Gone. Those two slices of Mediterranean pizza? Where the heck did they go? I am not sure I could even tell you what they tasted like. Eating is seriously one of my favorite activities. It's just so yummy and enjoyable. Why would I intentionally miss out on that experience, *especially* for something that might be stressful, numbing, or meaningless? For me, it's just a bad habit.

2. **I don't notice when I'm full and eat too much.** If I try to multitask when I'm eating, I totally miss my body's subtle cues that I've had enough. Suddenly, I'm doubled over in abdominal discomfort because I was comfortably full a while ago, but I was too busy watching the last five minutes of that parkour video to notice.

3. **It's messy.** My keyboard gets all gummed up from my sticky food fingers, and that's yucky.

👍 Mindful Approach 6: Savor Eating

Separate tech time from food time. We know we don't divide our attention well, and food is awesome. It can be the most enjoyable part of our day, and we get to do it three times (or more, depending on your noshing habits!). Why not pay attention and bask in those moments?

While in some parts of the world it's common for families to sit down and enjoy meals as important times of day all on their own, much of the cultural pressure from marketing in the United States has moved more toward food as fuel (though of course this is not universally true). What might be the advantage of being fully present for our eating experience? Try out these mindful approaches to eating and see if you can answer that for yourself.

Scan to listen.

- **Make it the main event.** Put everything else aside (especially phones) and really focus on nourishing yourself and enjoying. If possible, choose a place that is peaceful. (I usually eat dinner with at least two children under four, so for me, sometimes I just have to shut my eyes and wait for the chaos to abate to take my next bite.)
- **Put it on a plate (or bowl, depending on the food).** Yes, even that granola bar. It helps with the joy of eating.
- **Tune in to your senses.** Food can be enjoyed with all five of our senses: sight, touch, smell, taste, and even hearing. Start to notice the colors of your food. The texture. The way the flavors change and meld together as you chew. Giving ourselves permission to savor the goodness of eating helps us enjoy it even more.
- **Slow down.** We often eat too fast. Slowing down not only helps you more fully enjoy, but it helps hunger and fullness cues from your belly make it up to your brain.
- **Invite in gratitude.** Getting to satisfy our basic human need of nourishment is something we can appreciate. We can think about all the people who were a part of preparing our food, whether it be a bar of chocolate or a fancy dinner. It didn't just magically appear in front of us.

👁 Hijack 7: Friend Time while Distracted

This one will take a moment of honest reflection. Are you in the habit of being on your phone while someone is trying to talk to you in person? Maybe you try the occasional up-and-down glance to make sure they feel seen. Maybe you nod along while you gaze at your phone. Or maybe you have a pet or a sibling who desperately wants your attention when you get home from school, but you are caught up in another world. I remember one of my students talking about how she felt bad when she realized her dog was begging for her attention while she was totally engrossed in social media.

It is easy to get caught up in the digital world, even while our friends are present. We are used to turning to digital distraction if there's a lull in the conversation. In a bigger group, we feel okay turning to our phones as long as *someone* is paying attention to whomever is speaking. Our family members often don't seem as important as whatever is happening on our phone. Even our pets suffer when they come to us for affection and we absentmindedly stroke their eyeballs on accident.

Consider how it feels when you are trying to communicate with someone who is clearly only half listening. Especially if it's about something important. Quality conversation requires a speaker and a listener to be fully present with each other. It requires space to allow ideas to form and be explored and expressed. Do you really want to talk about a recent breakup with someone who is scrolling through TikTok videos? The answer, for most of us, is no. Research has shown that people are less willing to talk about vulnerable things, and feel less connected, if a phone is out on the table, even if it is upside down and silenced.

👍 Mindful Approach 7: Focused Friend Time

Let's go over a few ways we can ensure that our attention isn't divided when we are with people we care about. After all, the greatest gift we can give is our full attention. Connection is a basic human need, and our full presence is what helps us feel connected.

First, consider making a pact with your friends that you will put phones away at specific times. Sometimes it takes an initial conversation to get everyone on the same page. One person I talked with said that at this point, if he doesn't have his phone out when he's with his friends, he feels awkward, because they all do. So it would take an intentional shift to change that dynamic. Maybe choose a time to eliminate phones that is low impact, like when you're going for a walk or playing a game. That way, the activity links you *and* the conversation can flow without the pressure of staring each other down.

Then it's about relaxing into what might initially feel uncomfortable: fully showing up. How do we fully show up? Part of it is just about setting an intention to do so. This is going to seem so simple, it's silly that I'm even typing it. When your friend is talking to you, you listen. Not to interrupt, not to one-up them, not to put them down, but just to hear them out. Mindful listening is listening completely. It is noticing when your mind has wandered and drawing it back. This is especially important if someone is sharing something meaningful to them. Sometimes we feel pressure to give advice or a great response, but even more important than that is just to let them know they've been heard. Try committing to really being with your people.

👁️ Hijack 8: Homeworking while Distracted

You are trying to memorize the quadratic equation when your phone lights up. A new text. You tell yourself you'll just check this one text, and then you end up texting back and forth for twenty minutes. And checking Snapchat and TikTok. And Instagram. And then you finally return to your math where you were doing . . . what, exactly? We've all been distracted by our technology. The problem is, when you are trying to do something that requires deep concentration, it can take up to twenty minutes to truly return your mind to a task! That's a lot of minutes when you are trying to buckle down and get through the work. If you just sat down and got through the work, you'd not only likely do a better job, but you would be free to use all the time banked from not being distracted.

👍 Mindful Approach 8: Head in the Game

Start by taking stock of what is already happening. Put a sticky note on your desk, kitchen counter, or wherever you do homework, and every time you notice you feel compelled to check your phone, open a new tab to Reddit, or play a round of *Tetris*, put a little check mark on the page. You might also notice other distractions that come into play. *Suddenly, I'm very hungry for a snack! Oh, I think the cat might need to be let in. . . . I'll just go down to see. Ugh . . . what is that flavor in my mouth? I definitely need to brush my teeth right now.* It's helpful to just start noticing when our attention is pulled away from the task at hand.

The next step might be to start noticing what happens when we don't react to it. What if I felt an urge to check my text messages and didn't do it? What if I noticed my need to watch a new YouTube video . . . and just didn't? Can you notice that urge, and let it pass? The more we practice this impulse control, the better we get at it.

Finally, to make the distractions less compelling, what obstacles can you put in the way of finding those distractions? Sometimes we need to break habits by making it harder to complete them. Can you put the phone in the other room while you toil through those equations? (Or if you must have it nearby, turn off the notifications and put it out of sight.) Can you take your computer offline while you work on that five-page paper, or at the very least, close any tab that isn't immediately relevant, or at the *very, very* least, put anything irrelevant in a minimized window at the bottom of your screen? That way, even if the urge strikes, you can't do it immediately. You actually have to pause and decide to go get the phone, or turn the Wi-Fi back on, or scroll down and click through the minimized windows to find the distraction. Part of what makes technology so compelling as a distraction is how effortless it is to switch in and out of it. So make it harder!

👁️ Hijack 9: Emotional Distraction

I once listened to a comedian who did a whole bit about how people are so afraid to experience any sense of dread or emotional discomfort that we immediately turn to technology. We can't handle boredom, frustration, anger, anxiety, sadness, or grief, so we desperately try to escape these feelings. He said that as soon as he felt even an inkling of sadness, he immediately went to his phone and texted fifty people, writing "hi" "hi" "hi" "hi" "hi," and waited for the responses to roll in, so he could be distracted from any feelings. He wasn't actually processing with any of these people; he was just taking the dopamine hits as they rolled in, to take the edge off.

Can you relate?

It's not a new phenomenon, our desire to escape hard emotions. Plenty of distractions have always been around. What is new is

Journal Prompt

What is the impact of technology on your life, both positive and negative?

the ease with which we can escape into news stories, images, and communication. Distraction is always in our pockets. What's new is platforms that are designed to steal our attention and keep it as long as possible. We *never* have to feel, if we don't want to, when we have this very engaging form of distraction so readily available.

What's the problem with that? Well, it takes a lot of energy to not think about a problem. And as we are actively trying not to think about something, a part of our brain is always thinking about it to keep it out of our consciousness. It's not actually gone. It's just lurking around the corner, waiting for an in.

When you don't allow yourself to fully experience an emotion, and you just ignore and distract, it's like putting a lid on top of a volcano. At some point, the lid is going to get blown off. Suddenly you are screaming at your sister for asking if you are done with the salt. Or maybe the lava will just leak out around the cracks and fissures at random times, so you walk around feeling slightly crummy and uneasy all the time. Our systems were built to be expressed, and we face very real mental and physical health consequences if we don't learn how to be with, and move through, hard feelings.

Mindful Approach 9: Sit with Your Feelings

Don't get me wrong. Sometimes distraction is a very skillful response to emotional pain. Wallowing or getting caught up in the churning of our minds isn't always helpful. Sometimes we need an escape, and sometimes technology provides a healthy way out.

That said, this same comedian goes on to talk about how he was driving down the road when a beautifully sad song came on the radio, and he was overcome with emotion. He pulled to the side of the road and let himself cry. He didn't just sniffle. He bawled. And you know what he felt afterward? Relief. Calm. If you've ever had a good, complete cry, you can probably relate to this.

Here's the practice: feel your feelings. The next time you feel even a little antsy, bored, or frustrated, don't immediately reach for your phone. This might happen while you are in the car, waiting for your dinner to be ready, or sitting on the toilet. Investigate what your feelings actually feel like during this time. Where are they in your body? What sensations do you experience? (Do you feel tight or loose? Cold or hot? Itchy or tingly?)

When we do this exercise, the emotion sometimes builds and gets more intense. It gets harder to stay with it. What might happen if you stay with it a moment longer? You might use some deep breathing (see page 137). You might try to speak kindly to yourself in those moments, as you would with a good friend. A friend of mine has taken to calling herself "sweetheart" during tougher moments. If you can get over the cheesiness, what might your nickname for yourself be when times feel hard?

If you keep gently staying with your emotions—not forcing them away, ignoring them, or arguing with them—they'll move through on their own. In their own time. What does it feel like to be on the other side? To have done it?

Note: If you are frequently experiencing strong or difficult emotions, you might need some support in this process of staying with those feelings. Therapists are a great resource to help you learn how to be with your emotions and prove to yourself that you can do it.

👁 Hijack 10: Impulse Checking

There's a normal degree of checking our technology, and then there's obsessive, unhealthy checking. I would imagine that if you stopped and reflected for a minute, you would probably be able to quickly identify where you fall on this spectrum. This theme came up quite a bit in discussions with my students of all ages. Molly said, "It can be like a habit. For example, if I'm doing something else that doesn't include my phone, I find myself checking it probably every two minutes." I would imagine that for at least some of you, that sounds familiar. The impulse to pick up the phone is just too strong to resist, and we find ourselves picking up our phone again, and again, and again, just to check. Just to see. Just to compare. We can see the way many of the strategies used by tech companies really do impact us—the notifications, tags, likes, comments, streaks, rewards, and punishments all keep us coming back for more.

Mindful Approach 10: Investigate Impulse

By definition, impulses are strong urges that we follow without thought. So what happens when we stop and start to explore what it's really like to have an impulse?

Scan to listen.

Set aside a time for yourself to really explore what an impulse feels like in the body. Put your phone on the table in front of you, screen down, sound on. Now, notice when the first wave hits. When you feel the urge to pick it up.

What does it feel like? Is it fidgety? Tight? Electric? Is it in the head? Muscles?

What happens when you don't do anything about it? Does it build? Get more uncomfortable? Can you stay with it? Keep the breath long and deep as you explore the rising of that impulse.

If you stick with it long enough, you may experience something amazing. No matter how big and strong the urge gets, it also recedes. And then you've made it. You've ridden the wave. Do this enough and you may start to build confidence in your ability to not react to every impulse.

👁 Hijack 11: Trigger Thumbs

After third period, you reach into your bag and pull out your phone. On it are a series of text messages from your mom that look like this:

(10:34 a.m.)

Mom: K, when you get a chance, could you let me know your plans for dinner tonight?

(10:40 a.m.)

Mom: Because I'm trying to figure out if I need to include you in the menu, and I'm at the grocery store now. So I need to know now.

(10:55 a.m.)

Mom: Babe? Are you okay? I haven't heard anything so I'm starting to worry . . .

(10:57 a.m.)

Mom: Hello?

WTF? There are lots of things you'd like to shoot back to your mom, like a series of expletives for being so ridiculous. And a rant about how she *always* does this and it's so annoying! It's not that we are in the wrong to feel put out, but is there a better way to react? Can we ride out the impulse to shoot back a message and see what our more settled self might have to say?

Online communication offers a lot of opportunities to respond in ways that are careless, defensive, or mean. We often receive messages when we are trying to do something else, and if the tone of the message is in any way sideways, it's so easy to shoot something back without much thought or intention. Think for a minute: How many misunderstandings, or even arguments, could have been avoided with friends, family, or even strangers if one or both of you had waited three beats to respond?

👍 Mindful Approach 11: Pause, Breathe, Relax

I know, I know. It can be hard to stomach someone telling you, "Take three deep breaths." Honestly, if someone were to try to tell me that in the moment that I was pissed, I would only become more fired up and likely to explode. So why are we always told this?

Well, it turns out, it's a really effective strategy. First of all, it forces us to pause and do something other than think about how mad we are. It takes our minds out of rage mode and gives us something neutral to focus on. Second, our breath is directly linked to our nervous system. When we are anxious or angry or overwhelmed, our breath tends to be shallow and quick. It originates in our upper chest. This forms a feedback loop with our brain, so when we feel that kind of breathing, we feel more [*insert uncomfortable emotion here*], which in turn makes our breathing faster and harder. In prehistoric times, this reaction was really helpful as our bodies switched into fight, flight, or freeze mode and we prepared to run away or attack our predator. But you don't need this defensive mode to discuss your feelings. So how do you get out of it?

To short-circuit this feedback loop, you can intervene at the level of your body. It can be hard to talk yourself out of a difficult emotion when you are really revved up. If you intentionally slow down your breath, inhaling all the way into the belly and exhaling long and slow, this signals to the brain that you're okay. You don't need to attack. You don't need to run away. Even just three deep breaths have been shown to decrease breath rate (duh), heart rate, blood pressure, and muscle tension.

Additionally, when we are in fight, flight, or freeze mode, our whole body tenses up in preparation for action. We can again work from the level of the body to intentionally counter this tension by relaxing the areas where we hold stress. Let go in the forehead, jaw, and shoulders. Release in the arms, torso, and legs.

So, there's your lengthy explanation for a simple piece of advice: **Pause, breathe, relax.**

Try it. Right now. Stop what you are doing. Literally stop moving your body. Take three deep breaths into the belly and exhale slowly. Intentionally relax the body. See if you can notice even the slightest shift.

Scan to listen.

Then you can reconnect with your rational mind. Then you can consider how best to respond, maybe in person instead of via text, or decide if you even need to say anything at all.

👁️ Hijack 12: Texting over Talking

Let's just say it: It's so much easier to have hard conversations via text or messaging than in person. It's hard to look someone in the eye and tell them how you feel. It's hard to receive feedback that something you did might have hurt someone else, especially when you care about them. Having the hard conversation via text means we don't have to hear, or share, anyone's emotional state. We can hide our voice cracking, our eyes welling up with tears, or our reddening face. We can slow down and take time to carefully craft a message. We can add emojis to lighten the mood.

What we gain, no doubt, is ease.

But what do we lose?

When we communicate via text, we miss body language and tone, both considered hugely important for understanding meaning. We miss sarcasm, sighs, and crossed arms. We miss the very things we may seek to hide. If the point of having a conversation is to get to a place of mutual understanding, text messaging can make that harder.

Furthermore, despite being the most hyper-connected society in history, we are incredibly lonely. Studies show that even as more and more teens get phones, an increasing percentage of you say you feel lonely (more than any other generation, in fact). This makes sense because members of Gen Z (y'all born between 1997 and 2021) are spending less time face-to-face than teens used to in previous generations. And social media isn't helping. In a study done prior to the COVID-19 pandemic, those who were spending more time on social media (over two hours a day) were feeling more isolated than those who were spending less time (under half an hour). To be fair, it also seems like social media use isn't increasing feelings of isolation as long as people are also getting plenty of in-person time.

Yes, but having in-person conversations, especially involving conflict, is so . . . hard.

Yeah, it is. It's hard to be vulnerable with someone else. It's hard to see someone else's pain. And quite frankly, many of us aren't very good at it. But I would argue that doing hard things is good for us. It's how we grow as individuals and in our relationships.

Mindful Approach 12: Face-to-Face It Anyway

The way we build connections and real relationships is to be with people. To see them when they aren't hiding or curating, but just saying it like it is for them. To share ourselves, unedited and authentic. To learn that other people will care for us, even when we are not at our prettiest, best, brightest. It won't be easier. It will probably be messier. But it's worth it.

When you are called on to have those hard conversations, try it on. Face-to-face, assuming this conversation is with someone with whom you do not have safety concerns. Choose a time that you have both decided on. Then follow the tips below for an honest, productive conversation:

1. **Know thyself.** Before speaking, see if you can figure out your honest emotions and thoughts about what you need to discuss. Can you distinguish what you observe (facts) from what you think about what you see (evaluation or judgment)?
2. **Connect and stay connected.** Stay connected to the feelings in your feet, and your breath, as a way of not getting knocked off center.
3. **Speak.** Before saying anything, consider:
    ◦ Is it true?
    ◦ Is it kind?
    ◦ Is it necessary or helpful?

4. **Listen.** (Why is it so hard to just listen?) Put all your focus on whoever is speaking to you. See if you can listen with an intent to really understand the other person and not to argue, give advice, or win the discussion. Notice when your mind wanders and bring it back to listening.

5. **Respond.**
   ○ **Don't interrupt.**
   ○ **Clarify.** When the other person is done speaking, check to make sure you understand what they said. Maybe try, "It sounds like . . ."
   ○ **Confirm.** Ask if you understood correctly. You could ask, "Is that correct?"

6. **Build understanding.** Be clear about what you might want or need from the other person moving forward.

If you ever really want to nerd out on this, check out Oren Jay Sofer's book *Say What You Mean: A Mindful Approach to Nonviolent Communication.* He offers a lot of ideas about how to think about and practice this work.

◉ Hijack 13: Selfies and Self-Esteem

Have you ever noticed that after too much time scrolling, you suddenly feel like your life is crap? *That person is so perfect with their perfect teeth and perfect partner. And this person gets to travel the world with their family, while I am home in central Maine with nothing to see but miles of pine forest. How did that person get so dang flexible?* And then there's a layer of needing to present yourself in a particular way to keep up or best these people. As eighth grader Madelyn describes it, "It's the constant need of reassurance. The constant feeling of comparing yourself to other people, some people you don't even know. When we have a platform, or a feed, it immediately gets compared to other feeds. 'You can express yourself and be yourself on your own feed' they say, but it just makes you want to be less of yourself. I find myself constantly checking my likes, views, follows, etc. It's honestly tiring." We may start to see the lives of others, and the feedback we get on our photos and videos, as a measuring stick for our own lives.

Even when we *know* filters are a thing and people are taking a million shots and only posting the most amazing moments of their life, we can't quite seem to shake the feeling that they have their lives together and we don't. Eighth grader Elena reflects, "Though technology can be useful, it can also be problematic. Photoshop, body image, and perfection can all be seen through social media. We don't realize what we see on the social media is not always one and the same. People spend entire lives waiting for the 'perfect life' to come and knock on their door, but if there is anything I know as an aware teenager, it's that no child, no adult, no one, has a perfect life. Children and adults compare, and it's easy for human beings to be deceived by social media and believe that they are once again not accepted."

Even more alarming is the impact that using filters on our own pictures can have on our self-image. Some users start to believe that they should actually look like they do in their photos. Indeed, experts have coined the term *selfie dysmorphia* to discuss the crappy feelings people can have toward themselves because of internalized pressure to look like their filtered self. Some have taken it so far as to request plastic surgery that will make their actual face look like their filtered face. Something about this being a documented phenomenon shows me it's worth paying attention to.

The fact is, we don't even always notice what our minds are up to. It might not be obvious that when I look at a picture, I feel bad about myself. But if we constantly surround ourselves with pictures of people in their moments of glory, it can make our lives seem dull, ordinary, and boring by comparison. If we are pining after pictures of ourselves that we've filtered the crap out of, it can make our faces seem too round, flat, discolored, or hairy. It can make us feel bad about our strong, beautiful bodies that do so much for us. And that's not useful or healthy. In fact, it conveniently makes us more susceptible to those trying to tell us they can "fix" us with their product. So beware.

🖒 Mindful Approach 13: Delete, Delete, Delete

First, can you start to notice the fleeting habits of mind? This can be tricky to observe, but before you log on to a social media account, set an intention to notice what narrative your mind uses to respond to different photos and videos. Also, notice how your body responds. Is there a tiny stab of jealousy in the pit of your stomach? A slight tensing of muscles or a sucking-in of your cheeks? When you notice a friend's unflattering photo, do you secretly rejoice? (Be honest.) If your answer to any of these is yes, there's nothing wrong with you. In fact, congratulations, you noticed a common habit of mind: the comparing mind! We are less under the control of these mind states if we start to notice them when they are happening. We can say, *Hmm, I hear you, but I don't have to listen to you. I don't have to believe you.*

Sometimes, we start to realize it's not enough just to notice, and maybe we want to change our habits in the face of this revelation. In fact, part of my own movement away from spending lots of time on social media was that I didn't like how my mind responded to the images I was seeing. I finally saw how weird I was getting about looking at pictures of a long-ago friend doing yoga on exotic beaches in skimpy bikinis. I realized how my heart felt when I saw nearby friends doing something together, without me! The noticing was enough for me to say, *I don't actually want to feel that way. I don't want to invite in the opportunity to feel envious or jealous, especially when I know that what I am jealous of is moments of someone's life, not at all encompassing the specifics of their days and life experiences.* The noticing is what helped me make different choices. Because it's hard enough to love myself. I don't need more reasons to doubt. You might try limiting or even taking brief sabbaticals from social media platforms to notice the difference.

👁️ Hijack 14: Fear of Missing Out (FOMO)

Fear of missing out is real. Almost nothing is as painful as being stuck at home babysitting on a Saturday night, looking at pictures of your friends out doing something without you. Or have you ever been hanging out with one group of friends, gone to the bathroom, checked Instagram, and realized a whole slew of your classmates were having a party that same night? And even though you were just having a great time making massive ice cream sundaes and playing Taboo, you suddenly felt like the lamest? Something will always look more fun, exciting, or compelling than the thing you are doing. Always.

👍 Mindful Approach 14: Return to Now

First, own your fear. *I am afraid of missing out, dang it. I want to be liked and invited to cool things and have fun all the time.* We don't have to pretend we are above that. It's very much human nature to want social connection. Let's not fake otherwise. We would just be lying to ourselves, and that doesn't get us anywhere.

Second, notice the story your mind makes up around that feeling. Notice how the thing you were doing, which moments ago seemed totally fine, now seems lame and worthless. Perhaps you are thinking something like, *This sucks. I'd be way happier if I was out with my friends. They all are having an amazing time and I'm stuck at home.* Acknowledge that these are stories—powerful stories, but stories nonetheless. Stories that your mind made up, even if it was just subconsciously. Ask yourself, *Is there a different story I could tell here?* Notice whether anything comes up.

Third, come back to what's actually happening in front of you. Now that you are aware of what you are *not* doing, can you pay attention to what you *are* doing? Maybe it is something low-key, like game night with your family or ice cream sundaes with your best friends. These can be nice experiences, if we bring our whole attention back to the moment. This is the moment that is actually happening in our life, after all, so why not invest in being there for it?

Finally, start noticing when and how often FOMO happens. Maybe there are certain times when you know this feeling will be triggered by checking your phone. Make a pact with yourself about times when you are not going to look at Instagram or Snapchat. Be intentional about leaving your phone put away, even when you hit up the bathroom. Notice how that changes your experience of the time you are actually having.

Alert: You might notice a draw to check the phone. This feeling can be uncomfortable, especially in the beginning. Can you notice this urge without reacting? The more often you don't immediately react, the easier it will become to not react in the future. (Go back to Hijack 10: Impulse Checking, on page 134, for more on this.)

Hijack 15: Private Goes Public

Have you ever had that experience of getting a notification that someone has posted a picture of you, and your stomach drops? It can be so unnerving that anyone can share anything they want about you for the whole world to see (though our minds likely exaggerate the reach and impact of these posts). Regardless of the person's intention—whether it was playful, ignorant, or actually intended as cruel—a post can land painfully if it's not something you want shared. Perhaps it's an unfiltered photo of you in your jammies when you still have a little drool crusted on the corner of your mouth. Or maybe it's something much more serious, like an explicit photo you sent to someone privately. Whatever it is, if the poster didn't ask your permission before posting, this violation of trust can make us feel powerless, betrayed, and vulnerable.

Mindful Approach 15: Action Steps

Perhaps you'll start by just owning that it hurts when someone posts something about you that you didn't want shared. Let those feelings wash over you. Consider telling someone you trust about it and ask them to just listen. You don't need to argue with the hurt or make it better right away. Just start with, *Yeah, that really sucks.*

If it was someone you have a trusted relationship with, your next step may be to approach that person and tell them how it landed. "Hey, Aunt Sue, that Facebook picture of all the cousins first thing in the morning after our sleepover makes me feel embarrassed and exposed. Would you please take it down?"

Ideally, the person who posted is a decent human being, will realize the error of their ways, and quickly do what you ask.

However, if the content is something much more explosive, like a sext you sent your former boyfriend, that might be a hard one to handle yourself. Talk with your parents or a trusted adult about whether and how to approach that person and their family to discuss the violation and whether your family should involve law enforcement.

One of the most important gifts mindfulness can offer us is clarity. Pretending something doesn't hurt us or bother us serves nobody. In fact, when we bury these kinds of feelings, they don't go away. Instead, they tend to pop out sideways at other moments in our lives because they are unresolved. Make sure you are being honest with yourself. Mindful awareness can help you be courageous in your action steps.

👁 Hijack 16: So You Wanna Be an Influencer

It is part of the human condition to want to be known and appreciated. We want to have power and influence over others. Social media provides us with a whole host of ways to do that. There are some circles of influence within our friend groups and school communities, and then there are those that have transcended that inner circle and impact wider networks. Start by examining your own aspirations of power and influence. Are you producing content to gain followers, make an impact, and be seen? Are you hoping for a degree of fame?

According to a recent study, social media and YouTube influencers are among the top five career choices for people between the ages of eleven and sixteen. So if this is an aspiration for you, you aren't alone. And it can look so glamorous and appealing from where we normal folks sit. If you are recognizing this in yourself, it is wise to slow down and look at what you think you might get out of your stardom, and if that's really the best way to meet your needs.

🖐 Mindful Approach 16: Dig Deep

I am not actually here to tell you whether you should or shouldn't try to be an influencer (on a small or large scale). I am here to challenge you to consider whether this dream lines up with your values (or not). Go back to page 96 and reconnect with what is important to you and what you care about. Then consider whether your drive to become an influencer helps you live in alignment with those values.

Does this goal allow you to share powerful messages about amazing work you are doing and inspire others to do the same? Are you looking for an easy way to make money? Do you think having a lot of followers will make you feel better about yourself? Are you trying to help people lighten up and laugh a little? Maybe some combination of all four? Check in with yourself about that before you dump a bunch of time or attention into this pursuit. *What do I think being an influencer will give me? Might I be wrong?*

One way we can investigate this is through a journaling exercise we will call the Repeating Why. Write the question, *Why do I want to be an influencer?* Then freewrite everything that bubbles up in your mind. When there's nothing else to write, ask again, "Why do I want to be an influencer?" Notice what comes up this time and freewrite until there is nothing else. And then again. And again, until you feel you've truly exhausted your responses. This can be helpful to identify and acknowledge the many motives that might be driving your desires (even those that may feel less noble). Having a deeper sense of our personal *why* can help us check that against our values and decide if this is something we really want for ourselves.

We may mistakenly believe that if we achieve a certain amount of influence, it will alleviate some struggles we have with our own identity. It will make us feel more confident in ourselves, happier, more content with our lives. But seeking validation outside of ourselves almost always

Practice of Self-Acceptance

Scan to listen.

What might it look like to practice self-acceptance? Let's give it a try.

Allow your eyes to close. Sit with confidence and comfort, so that the spine is long but the muscles are relaxed. Notice the breath moving in and out of the body.

When you are ready, try saying or thinking the following phrases:

"I am content with myself just the way I am.
I don't have to prove myself to anyone.
I don't have to be better.
If I can't believe that in this moment, I may sometime in the future."

Repeat these phrases a few times to yourself, slowly. See if you can let them sink in. When you are ready, let your eyes open and return to your present moment.

How was that? Maybe you experienced a tiny bit of relief with that reminder. Maybe you noticed a ton of resistance. If so, this practice is probably for you! It means you are not in the habit of thinking kindly toward yourself. *Especially* if this was hard, I challenge you to try it every day for a month and see what happens. Can you move the needle even the slightest bit closer to self-love? Can you move it even the slightest bit away from needing that validation from others?

falls flat. Because what we actually need is self-acceptance and a little self-love. This can be harder to achieve than amassing thousands of followers, but ultimately this affirmation of ourselves is what may fulfill us.

👁️ Hijack 17: Biting at Clickbait

"You'll never believe what this woman found under her bed!"

Click.

"Do these five things as a teen and you will be rich by your thirtieth birthday!"

Click.

"Celebrities swear by this one fitness move . . ."

Click.

Just as a fish is attracted to bait on a lure, humans are attracted to headlines that are outlandish, improbable, and infuriating. The more something ruffles our emotional feathers, the more we want to learn about it. Some news organizations are at least partly motivated to share information and educate the public. And other news organizations are simply trying to rile us up to win our attention. Our brains crave novelty and are attracted to emotionally charged experiences, so when we see something that seems unlikely or maddening, we *need* to know more. It is so easy to get sideswiped by these clickbait headlines and find ourselves off on some online tangent.

👍 Mindful Approach 17: Notice the Click

The first thing we can do is prime ourselves with the understanding that clickbait headlines are designed to capture our attention and draw us in.

Knowing this makes us less susceptible to the lure (though it will still have its draw). You might want to remind yourself of this by placing a sticky note reading, "Don't believe everything you see" at the top of your computer screen. You can also vet news sources before visiting them, so you know which ones are more reliable. (The *New York Times* is more reliable than some random person's blog, for instance.) This practice can help keep you from clicking on any old thing.

Then, armed with this knowledge, start to notice what sensations arise when you read particularly provocative headlines. Let's go back to the headlines that started this section. Read the following headline, pause for a few moments, and notice how it lands in your body.

"You'll never believe what this woman found under her bed!"

Maybe you get a fascinated feeling, one of being physically drawn in. I notice my mind goes, *What* is *under her bed?* The headline plays with our childhood fears of something being under our beds. I made this headline up and yet, there's still a part of me that wants to know the answer!

How about this one?

"Do these five things as a teen and you will be rich by your thirtieth birthday!"

Is there a longing that happens here? Almost a physical drawing forward of your body? Even if we know it's probably BS, what if it's not? (Side note: if you do happen to know what those five things are, please send them to me so I can write this article and my kids can be rich.)

Finally, if you do click the headline, what does it feel like to read the story? Was it exciting? A letdown? Are you able to read it with a critical eye? Start to notice how the headlines get you, and if you ultimately gain anything from your *click*!

👁️ Hijack 18: Tech Guilt

One thing we might start to notice as we build awareness around our tech habits is that we feel bad about them. We might be surprised by how much of our lives we have ceded to tech giants. We may feel guilt when we ignore important parts of our lives in favor of going deep down into the tech rabbit hole. Guilt isn't necessarily a bad thing. It is a good clue as to what our heart and mind want, and it might inform us that our tech habits are not serving us. But guilt can also be crippling, and if it becomes too overwhelming or painful, we might choose to stop looking at our behaviors and feelings.

Mindful Approach 18: Simply Begin Again

With mindfulness, every moment is an opportunity to begin again. It is an invitation to be curious, nonjudgmental, and even to take it all less personally. We can think about habits as having a great amount of momentum, like a giant boulder rolling down a hill. If we wake up and realize we don't like the direction that boulder is heading, and we try to stop it by simply standing in front of it, that's going to hurt like hell. It takes time, patience, and a sense of humor to really be able to look at ourselves honestly and make new choices. Slowing down the boulder, or changing its course, will not happen overnight.

This is especially true with technology, where it's not just our individual habits working against us, but our collective habits. Our whole society has become hooked. In working to set a new standard for ourselves, we are bound to fail. But we are also bound to have the opportunity to begin again.

Try these phrases:

- I will begin again.
- That was the best choice I could make at the time.
- I needed that, and now I have the freedom to make a new choice.
- Insert your own here:

It takes strength and courage to chart a new path. And you can do it.

CHAPTER 7

Living Your Best Life

Close your eyes. Okay, I guess you have to read through this first, but then come back and close your eyes and walk yourself through this exercise (or listen to the recordings on the website).

Scan to listen.

Imagine yourself waking up on your most perfect day. What does it feel like to be in bed? How do you soak in that moment? Do you stay there for a while to enjoy the restfulness? Are you someone who loves to jump right up and throw on some upbeat music? Whatever those first few moments in your ideal day look like, imagine them.

Then imagine what it would be like to head for breakfast. What do you eat? Who is with you? What's the weather like outside?

Next, picture your morning. Do you stay home and lounge around in your PJs, cuddling your puppy? Do you head out to shoot hoops with friends? Do you climb a mountain with your family? Imagine what it feels like to be doing whatever it is that you've chosen. Energizing? Calming and soothing?

Now it's lunch time! Do you eat out? Come home? Do you have sandwiches? Soup? Pasta? Tacos? Do you finish up with dessert?

Afternoon rolls around. What now? Do you go out for a walk? Take a catnap in a sunny patch on the couch? Hit the beach or slopes?

Volunteer with Habitat for Humanity? What are you loving at that time? Who is with you?

Evening comes and you are getting hungry. Another opportunity to chow down! Are you going to hit up a restaurant? Eat your dad's famous potpie? What meal would be nourishing and perfect for you?

How will you wind down from your day? Watch a movie with your family? Read a book curled up in your beanbag chair? Take a short walk around the block?

Finally, once you've completed your bedtime routine, how does it feel to get into bed? How does it feel to have lived through this perfect day?

When you are ready, come back to the present.

This is an idealizing exercise. Obviously, we don't usually have this much control over every moment of the day. We must consider other people's needs. And we do things—school, homework, practice, and so on—that may not feel gratifying in the moment but may ultimately serve us. Some life circumstances simply do not allow for us to do all that we wish. But it can be really helpful to know in our bodies what it feels like to live a beautiful day, as well as what factors help create those feelings.

Journal Prompt

Consider what an ideal day might look for you. Write it out in as much detail as you can, including technology as part of that picture to the extent that you would want it there. What will you do? *How* will you do it? How will you feel?

This exercise is meant to highlight the fact that how you spend your time matters. What you fill your mind with—experiences, content, images—matters. It may be the most important thing to consider. The way we spend each moment ultimately adds up to our lives. If we really want to start being clear about how our tech can best serve us, we need to be very clear about what we want it to serve. Many people grapple with this big question their whole lives: *What work, activities, causes, and ways of being in the world make me feel most alive, most connected, and most authentically myself?* There will not be a final answer to this question. It will be a lifelong inquiry, and your response will undoubtedly shift as you grow and have new priorities.

Setting Your North Star

This kind of idealization exercise helps us set our North Star. The North Star was a guiding star for sailors before the age of GPS. Crews would set their course by it, and though they were sometimes blown off by high winds, choppy seas, or storms, they could also use the North Star to reorient themselves when the clouds cleared.

We need a metaphorical North Star to understand what kind of life we are trying to create for ourselves. In the perfect-day exercise, what were the qualities that made that day so magnificent? Was it that it felt spacious? That you felt connection? That you cared for others? That you laughed and found humor? In all likelihood, you probably dreamed up a day in which you were living out some of your values. You can see concretely what brings you joy. Envisioning those things helps us get a sense of what we might want to prioritize, given the time in our control. We can set ourselves up to at least head in the direction of happiness and fulfillment, knowing that many elements are outside of our control and may push us off course.

If you have no North Star, you just sort of get aimlessly tossed about by whatever comes your way. You have nothing you are working to create for yourself. You are letting the fates decide. Having a North Star doesn't mean we get rigid about anything. We don't want to hold too tightly to it, as there may be great lessons learned, and even new destinations discovered, if we accept challenges and course shifts along the way. So even as we set a course, can we embrace that there will be side trips and maybe even a new plot set, based on what comes up as we go?

When I was in middle and early high school, the thing that made me feel most accomplished, satisfied, and alive was gymnastics. I loved the discipline, the ruthless workouts, and the strength I felt in my body. I loved the commitment and precision this sport required. I loved the structure. To be honest, I was never very good. It wasn't about being the best. It was about being in my body and making progress through effort. It was about working hard alongside others to be a strong team.

When I started getting injured repeatedly, and the back handsprings that I had been effortlessly throwing on beam suddenly made me balk in terror, I knew it was time to move on. That chapter closed. And I had to find new ways of making meaning in my life. While I spent some time experimenting with different experiences, I ultimately noticed that I found purpose and satisfaction in other things, including painting, being with family, and supporting others in connecting with themselves.

Finding meaning in our lives won't come just from what we do, but how we show up. Are we all the way there for those experiences? Or are we distracted? Can we find meaning and contentment even in moments that are not exciting, awe-inspiring, or fun?

We've spent a lot of time looking at our tech habits. (I mean, that *is* what this book is about!) But our tech habits do not exist in isolation. Sometimes they are a result of some unmet need in our lives. Sometimes our habits result in an unmet need. It helps to figure out what things nourish us and help us to feel most alive. Only then can we really understand how our tech use can support that.

While your own personal brand of humanness will dictate the

specifics of what brings you joy, contentment, and meaning, some life practices have universally been shown to support wellness. Our minds and bodies need certain things to be well.

If we think of our lives in terms of time, we want to be conscious of balancing how we are using our time. Are we meeting all our needs? What could we be doing to better nourish ourselves and our community? How can we use technology to support our engagement in these different kinds of time?

There's no magic number for how to balance our time. Again, it's going to depend on who you are, and it's a lifelong journey to figure out what works best for you at any given moment. Sometimes you'll need to shift and get more rest or more movement (my natural yearly rhythm dictates that I trend toward hibernation in the colder months and movement in the warmer ones). But it can help to begin with a framework that works most of the time. So how can we set up our lives so that we have time to nourish ourselves, and how can tech support us in doing so?

Reflection and Self-Discovery Time

How well do you know yourself? Seems like it should be an easy answer, right? But to know ourselves, we must pay attention. We need to make space in our lives to observe and be, without constant input or requirements to perform. If we are always busy racing around, performing for others and taking in content, we can't really get a sense of our true wants and needs. How can we see our patterns of thought? Here are a few things to try:

Journaling. While the world of social media invites us to externalize and share all aspects of our life experiences, journaling is a way of exploring thoughts and emotions internally, without broadcasting them to the world at large. No performance or editing is required. It gives you space to explore, take risks, and mess up, without an audience. Private spaces are critical to self-understanding.

A few journaling strategies follow.

- **Morning pages.** In her book *The Artist's Way*, Julia Cameron encourages readers to sit down first thing in the morning and write three unedited pages, longhand.
- **Gratitude journal.** Create a list of things you felt grateful for during the day. Look especially for smaller, less flashy moments, like laughing with a friend, that first bite of granola in the morning, or a hot shower at the end of the day.
- **Hard stuff.** Consider writing about the hard stuff as it comes up—the stuff that plagues your mind and won't let go. This might help you face and unravel some of the difficulty and give you more space to breathe. But beware of getting stuck. Consider changing tactics if this practice feels obsessive or unproductive.

Solo dates. Take yourself on a date! Go see a movie. Marvel at the fall leaves. Visit a museum. Grab a cup of hot chocolate at the local coffee shop. Take some time by yourself to do something that feels nourishing to you. It might feel awkward at first to do these things solo, but over time, notice the freedom of not having to come up with anything to say for a little while. Focus on how the experience feels for you. What can you learn from doing an activity by yourself?

Autobiography. If someone were to ask you, "How did you get here? What makes you tick? Why are you the way you are?" how might you answer? Taking uninterrupted time to share our stories can be incredibly powerful. It gives us the opportunity to step back and reflect on our lives. This is something we can do as a journaling exercise, or, even more powerfully, as a conversation with friends and family.

If you choose to have this conversation with your people, it can be helpful to set up a structure for the share, like a hot-seat model. In this model, everyone sits together in a circle. (You could also do this one-on-one.) One person is put on the "hot seat," and everyone else is there just as listeners. The "hot seater" simply shares what comes up for them in response to the guiding question. There is room for silence, to allow the hot seater space to reflect, and the listeners are there to fully hear the speaker. They don't need to say anything at all, except when the hot seater is done speaking. At this point, listeners can share what they appreciated about what they heard and the experience in general.

How Tech Can Help

Many of these exercises are about taking time away from tech to connect to oneself. But you could also use tech to support these endeavors. Just be mindful of how you do so. You could journal on your computer, but to really allow some uninterrupted time, you'd probably want to make sure you aren't connected to the internet. If speaking your thoughts works better for you, you might try an audio journal. You could use your phone to try out meditation apps, but you'd probably want to make sure that notifications are off (or at least silenced).

Downtime

Sometimes, the best thing we can offer ourselves is nothing. We benefit from simply having space in our day. We live in a culture of productivity, where downtime is not really practiced. But we cannot handle constant input and output without depleting our reserves. What might it be like to experiment with lying on a hammock? Getting under a cozy blanket on the couch? Coming home from school and simply crashing on your bed for a few minutes? Don't look at your phone. Don't chat with a friend. Don't go for a brisk walk. If you're not used to this, it can be unnerving. "I must do *something*," you may find yourself saying. It might be worth setting a timer, even for just one minute, and working your way up. Truly, just be.

Furthermore, some of our best ideas can grow from downtime. I have childhood memories of driving from Massachusetts to Maryland to see my grandparents, and for many of those ten hours in the car, I would just stare out the side window, thinking and daydreaming, not about anything in particular. It was an opportunity to create more space to think creatively and freely and without reservation. The more space, the more outlandish and creative my thoughts would get. These are the conditions for *Eureka!* moments, when we have a sudden revelation about the nature of life that makes us feel awed and inspired. (I remember that it suddenly occurred to me when I was ten that perhaps we didn't all see color the same way. *Gasp!* I couldn't believe this possible truth.) Mark Beeman, coauthor of *The Eureka Factor*, says "activities that are too demanding of our brain or attention—checking email, reading the news, watching TV, listening to podcasts, texting a friend, etc.—tend to stifle the kind of background thinking or mind-wandering that leads to creative inspiration." We need brain breaks to let things percolate.

Mindful Practice to Try

Scan to listen.

A mindfulness practice called open awareness involves simply taking note of whatever arises in our present experience. So, as I sit here, I hear and see a car driving by. I notice the pressure of my right leg crossed over my left. I feel pressure behind my forehead. I think, *Uh-oh. Headache.* Maybe I need to get off my screen soon. My throat feels sore. I have an urge to drink some tea.

Starting with a timer set for one minute, let yourself zone out and notice what naturally arises. Don't interfere. Don't try to change. Just notice as sounds, thoughts, and emotions drift in and out. There it is, and then it's gone. There it is, and then something stronger captures my attention. Allow yourself to just be an observer, rather than a doer.

We can also create conditions for this kind of mind space by doing a mundane task, like gardening, raking leaves, or cleaning our rooms. When we do something physical but not mentally demanding, that creates space for our minds to wander.

How Tech Can Help

Beyond setting a timer or finding a guided meditation on open awareness, I would highly recommend not using technology for this experience.

Sleep Time

Taking downtime one step further, let's mention sleep. We've talked about how technology frequently gets in the way of sleep and that teens are not getting the recommended eight to ten hours of it each night. Sometimes we may not even notice how sleep-deprived we are until we start getting enough. Knowing that school schedules are not built to support teens' natural sleep habits, how do you ensure that you get enough sleep?

For ideas about how to build healthy sleep habits, return to page 75 in chapter 3.

Mindful Practice to Try

Scan to listen.

We experience stress in our bodies, often as tension in our muscles. One way we can help ourselves deal with normal daily stressors is to intentionally relax body parts that might be tight. And one way we can help our bodies relax is through an exercise called squeeze and release. Let's try it.

Start by just noticing how your body feels right now. Check in with your jaw, your shoulders, your fists, your belly. Also notice how your mind is. Busy? Settled? Sleepy? Whatever you find, it's not bad! It's just information and we can see how little things we do may affect how we feel.

Next, notice your feet. As you breathe in, gently squeeze your feet, and as you breathe out, release them.

As you breathe in, squeeze your calf muscles, and as you breathe out, release.

Inhale and tense the muscles in your upper legs, and then exhale and let them go.

Squeeze your legs and feet all together as you breathe in, and release them as you breathe out.

Move up to your belly and engage your muscles there as you take a breath in, then breathe out and let go.

Do the same thing in the chest and shoulder blades as you breathe in and squeeze, and out to release.

Gently squeeze the muscles all down your arms and into your fists . . . and let go as you exhale.

On an inhale, tense the muscles in your neck and face, and let everything go on an exhale.

Now, engage your whole body. Tense it as you breathe in, and relax it as you breathe out.

Check in with your body and mind. Do you notice any shifts?

How Tech Can Help

Some people who have a really hard time going to sleep have found relief in listening to guided meditations like yoga nidra (progressive muscle relaxation like the one above). Others listen to sleep stories, in which stories are designed and told in such a way that they create a soothing experience for the listener. Still others might play some form of white noise through their devices. If you think you can have your technology in your sleep space without using it to scroll, text, or play games, these might be some ways of using your technology for good!

Nature Time

Humans need time outside. From an evolutionary perspective, we spent thousands of years in the elements, taking in natural settings. A whole movement called forest bathing (translated from *shinrin-yoku* in Japanese) involves people exploring the woods using their senses. The health benefits are well documented and wide-ranging, but this activity is particularly good at easing the symptoms of stress. Perhaps you already understand this to be true for yourself and spend time in nature. Or maybe time in nature is outside of your comfort zone. If so, there are ways to get an outdoors hit without rock climbing up the sheer face of El Capitan in Yosemite National Park.

You can start by just finding green spaces nearby. If you are deep in the city, this might mean consciously noticing trees and flower boxes or looking up to the sky to watch passing clouds. Or maybe you simply grow a tiny succulent in your window and take some time to observe it. If you are in a rural area, you might roam fields, mountains, or lakes. Whatever you have access to, can you use all your senses to really take in that natural element? Can you find a sense of the stillness and peace that the natural world offers?

Mindful Practice to Try: 360 Senses

Scan to listen.

Nature pulls us into the present moment in a way that often feels restful. We can enhance that awareness by intentionally staying with the sensations it gives us. These can include feeling the wind on our cheeks or the soft ground beneath our feet, hearing the trill of a bird, or smelling the scent of balsam or eucalyptus in the air.

Try the following practice the next time you're outside, choosing the senses that feel most nourishing to you.

Perhaps begin by using your eyes to take in your surroundings. Look up toward the sky and notice colors, shapes, and patterns. Slowly turn 360 degrees and look out as far as you can in every direction. Look down to take in the textures of the ground.

Next, shift from seeing to feeling. What does that same ground *feel* like underfoot? Consider taking some steps forward and notice the pressure on the soles of your feet. If it's warm enough, you can do this without shoes and really tune in to the sensations, such as tickling or temperature. Notice any sensations on the skin from the air around you. Is there a breeze? A gale? Can you feel the warmth of the sun? Is it blazing hot? How is your body taking in its surroundings?

Consider closing your eyes and tuning in to sound. What noises are happening around you? What sounds are far away from the body? Close to the body? If we lie down, what is different about what we can hear? Can you notice the silence that sits between sounds?

Is there a scent in the air? If so, what are its qualities? Without getting too bogged down in trying to figure out what it is, try to experience the qualities of that scent—sharp, acrid, subtle, clean, musky. Take it all in.

I'll leave taste up to you—if wintergreen or wild raspberries are in your area, you may enjoy exploring how those taste. (Be certain of what you're eating, though. Don't just put a random berry in your mouth.)

Notice what it felt like to really engage with your surroundings. How did it impact your body?

How Tech Can Help

You can look online to find parks or trail systems near you. What places in your area meet your outdoor desires? Do you want to climb a high peak? Do you want to lie on a blanket by the water? You might look at a map of the area around you and notice green spaces. Another possibility is to see what trail guides have to offer. Alltrails.com and Trailfinder.info are good places to start.

For inspiration, you might follow a local blogger or social media personality who loves getting outdoors. Some people also find it engaging to download an app that helps them identify and learn about the natural world as they move through it, such as a plant-identifying app. Simply knowing a plant's name can be a way of feeling more connected to it!

Food Time

While we used the metaphor of food to consider how we can create a healthy tech diet, we also need a healthy food diet. That means eating whole, nutrient-dense foods. As food journalist Michael Pollan says, "Eat food. Mostly plants. Not too much."

Our culture in the United States is a bit sick around food. Half the time we get messages telling us to eat big, greasy burgers and extra-large sodas for less money, and the rest of the time we hear that we should be on this or that diet because we are too fat from eating those burgers. Neither message is particularly helpful or true, and both are geared toward making us feel like we need something to feel better, whether it be unhealthy food or a diet plan.

What we actually need are delicious, whole foods including fruits, vegetables, protein sources (meat, dairy, beans, tofu, and so on), and whole grains. And we need time to eat these foods together—mealtimes when we sit down and enjoy company and breaking bread. Nearly every culture has traditions around mealtimes.

Of course, regarding both these needs, there are optimal conditions, and then there is reality. If we can't find fresh veggies, we may incorporate some frozen veggies into our diet. If we can't sit down for dinner together every night, we might find a time once a week to eat together. Think about what would make mealtime most nourishing to you in your context, and see if you can build that in.

Mindful Practice to Try

Mindful eating can help you to fully experience and savor your meal.

Scan to listen.

To the extent that it makes sense, start by making a beautiful arrangement of your food. This could be as simple as putting your popcorn in a pretty bowl or as complicated as creating carrot curls and artfully arranged vegetables on top of your salad.

Perhaps you'll give thanks for all that had to happen for you to get this food—to whoever purchased it for you, made it for you, grew it for you, brought it to you. To the sun, the soil, the plants, and the animals themselves. Just hold a sense of appreciation.

Next, simply look over the food in front of you. Notice its colors, shapes, and textures.

Inhale through the nose and notice what it smells like. Do this a few times.

Now, as you pick up your food or utensil, just notice how whatever you have in your hand feels.

Slowly lift the morsel and really pay attention to how it tastes as it lands in your mouth. Maybe even close your eyes as you chew and take in the various tastes in different parts of your mouth.

As you continue to eat, stay with the experience of eating. Notice any impulses to get up, to check your phone, to turn your attention away. Take a slow breath each time these impulses arise, and then return to eating.

How Tech Can Help

You can find a bajillion recipes online, and a bajillion and one recipe sites can help you learn how to prepare meals. YouTube also has many videos of top chefs demonstrating some of the techniques they use, as well as videos of cooking and baking competitions. Trying out new and creative ways of prepping meals can enhance your connection to the eating experience.

Creative Time

When we were wee ones, creativity was a natural part of the way we were in the world. We used to simply and spontaneously create, using play dough, markers, paint, scissors, sticks, rocks, pine cones, and other objects. Do you remember that joy of just making and moving? I watch my three-year-old unself-consciously slam her marker repeatedly on the page, smearing and clashing colors together, and then cover them all with a healthy topping of glue, just because she's curious to see what will happen. She dances along to songs, wildly swinging arms and legs, rolling around on the floor, and simply finding movement in response to the music. She doesn't care at all what it looks like. It just feels good.

Taking time for creativity allows us to feel free. It provides space for self-awareness and expression without self-consciousness. It can provide stress relief. We get to know ourselves better through experimenting and trying new things.

In a world when we are so quick to post and share, what would it be like to make some time just for you? Perhaps you will ultimately want to share something that grows from this messy, unobserved time, but maybe not. When we do some of this work away from the camera, recording device, or spotlight, then we can peel back some of the self-protective barriers we have developed. It's no longer about creating a thing others will like; it becomes about simply exploring what's in you.

Expressing oneself can take a variety of forms. We can paint, draw, play instruments, bake, dance, take photographs, make movies, craft, write, knit, sew, make jewelry, or about a million other pursuits. One thing that continuously impressed me as I interviewed students for this book was how creative they are, and that they've found so many ways to integrate technology into these pursuits.

Mindful Practice to Try

Scan to listen.

Two of the biggest stumbling blocks to creativity are the judgy-pants voice in our heads and distraction. A simple focusing and awareness practice can help get us ready for any creative pursuit. Starting with a body scan can help us focus our minds and invite the judgy-pants voice into the background where it doesn't run the show.

Try lying down for this exercise. Take a few deep breaths, intentionally lengthening the exhale. As you breathe out, imagine all the tension in your body draining out.

Now, draw your attention to the top of your head and notice sensations there.

Focus down into your face, around the eyes, cheeks, and jaw.

Notice the neck and shoulders. Invite any release you feel might be helpful. Mentally trace all the way down both arms into the hands.

Really take a moment with the hands, zooming in and feeling sensations there. Is there tingling? Warmth? Coolness? Linger here for a moment longer.

When the mind wanders, whether the thoughts are critical or harmless, see if you can gently refocus . . . *ahh, hands. What might I notice there?*

Now, come back up the arms and down into the torso, feeling into the chest as it naturally rises and falls with the breath.

Scan down into the belly and hips.

Now draw the attention further down into your upper legs, knees, lower legs, and feet.

See if you can have a sense of your whole body from head to toe. Open your eyes.

If, at any point during this exercise, you notice your mind starts bullying you, you don't have to respond to it at all. You can just turn your attention elsewhere. Let that voice naturally quiet as you don't feed it with your attention. Or confront the voice, turning right toward it and offering, "I hear you. It's okay," before returning to your body and the task at hand.

How Tech Can Help

As we discussed in chapter 1, tech can help us with both the creative process and sharing our final products. You may remember Evan and Jeremy, the brothers who have really made technology work for their creative processes. Evan spends tons of time away from tech, practicing guitar, sax, piano, and other instruments. Then he brings his music production online, where he can write music notation, record, edit, collaborate, and ultimately share his work. His cinephile brother Jeremy uses his technology to watch films, discuss them on subreddits, and then create his own content. Some of his work is for film classes and some for TikTok, and each of these projects allows him to explore his inner world, which he ultimately shares outward.

Mastery Time

Nothing is like the experience of mastering a difficult skill or concept. And school is not the only place where learning happens. You might work on mastering a back handspring (obvious example from my childhood), a challenging piano piece, juggling four oranges, or a really difficult math concept. The harder the skill, the more satisfying it is when we finally get it. Success requires a balance of focused, intentional time and space for mind roaming to allow the new learning to integrate into our long-term memory.

Let's say you are working on a free throw. The best thing you can do is practice and practice hard. (Kobe Bryant, one of the best basketball players of our time, was said to take anywhere from five hundred to one thousand jump shots a day in the off-season.) During practice time, you want to be all in, training your mind and body to make these shots effortlessly. And then a time will come when practice is no longer productive, when your mind and body need a break. Rest and sleep are not just a pause from mastering skills; they are an integral part of it. We can apply this to anything: from studying for that math test to mastering the saxophone. It takes focused work periods supported by restorative rest periods to achieve mastery.

You can also use visualization to help support learning a skill or building strength. Researchers have found that even just imagining you are playing a particular piano piece can help you build muscle memory in your fingers. And imagining that you are physically exercising can increase your physical fitness.

Mindful Practice to Try

If you are building a new skill, try adding an embodied visualization practice to your routine. As athlete and mindfulness coach Amy Saltzman describes in her book *A Still Quiet Place for Athletes*, can you try to actually feel yourself doing a particular move in your body as you imagine it?

Scan to listen.

Pick one aspect of a physical skill you are trying to master. Perhaps it is the underhand serve in a tennis match or that part of Tchaikovsky's "Piano Concerto No. 1" that you keep tripping up on. You may start by finding a video of a top athlete or performer doing that skill. As you watch, imagine that it is you doing it. Rather than just thinking about it, can you imagine the feeling in your body as you go through the movements? Then close your eyes and spend five minutes imagining that movement, over and over, repeated perfectly. Again, rather than just thinking, really imagine your body moving and how it feels. When paired with physical practice, this visualization can be a powerful way to improve your craft.

With this concept of mastery, more important than what you do is how you do it. Is your mind there for it? Engaged? Can you become totally absorbed in your learning and find that flow state where you don't even have to think about it anymore? When your body just takes over and you can witness your skill? This is an incredibly powerful feeling, and one worth working toward, no matter what you might be trying to achieve.

How Tech Can Help

The internet offers a treasure trove of expert videos—whether they're from artists, musicians, athletes, or even academics—so you can closely study what it looks like, sounds like, and maybe even feels like to do something with a high degree of skill. You might find inspiration from interviews with highly skilled folks about the blood, sweat, and tears they put in to get to the place where they make their abilities look effortless.

You might also use tech to record yourself completing a skill so that you can learn from your performance. When I went to running camp in high school, I remember the coaches used to record our gait, then had us watch the recording to notice the ways our running form was helping or getting in the way. Through this process, I learned how I was habitually holding my body, along with small changes I could make to become more efficient in my movements. Consider what is the equivalent in your life, and how you could use technology to hone a skill.

Physical Time

The mind-body connection is *real*. We need movement not only to be physically well, but to be mentally and emotionally healthy. That means figuring out how you will build movement into every day (well, nearly every day) is critical. The Centers for Disease Control and Prevention (CDC) says teens need one hour a day of physical activity that is moderate to vigorous in intensity, including activities that get your heart pumping, build muscle, and strengthen your bones.

If you look at the one-hour recommendation and say, "That's *it*?" because you already have hours of soccer practice after school, with conditioning built in, then you're probably good. And do remember that it is also possible to overdo it. If you exercise excessively and you're hyper-focused on weight loss or body image, you might actually benefit from dialing it back a bit. One of the tricky things here is that our bodies do need physical activity, but we don't want to fall prey to marketing ploys that tell us we need to be smaller, lighter, bulkier, or stronger, and that those marketers will sell us the thing to make up for our deficiencies.

If you look at that number and say, "Yowzah," do not be alarmed. You don't have to go from nothing to an hour immediately. Maybe you start with some walks around the block. Carve out ten or fifteen minutes to do a gentle yoga video. Try hiking up a hill near your home. Splash around in a pool. There are lots of ways to add movement, even if you don't identify as an athlete.

Mindful Practice to Try

This practice is intended to help with some of that body-shaming culture that we are all subject to. What if we started practicing healthy ways to think about ourselves? Cultural messaging is so strong in the other direction that we must actively work to find and grow the voice of self-love and acceptance.

Scan to listen.

Start in a comfortable, relaxed position. Have a sense of your body as a whole, and call to mind some of the ways it serves you. It allows you to take in the world through your senses. It tries to

Ten Ways to Exercise for People Who "Don't Exercise"

Maybe you are someone who really doesn't like sports, or who hates the idea of exercise, or who just doesn't know how to begin. Maybe you have some physical differences that make traditional exercise more challenging. We can get creative and think outside the box about ways we can move and strengthen our bodies that don't involve joining the varsity swim team.

1. Sit on a yoga ball, or stack some books to create a DIY standing desk, while doing your homework.
2. Park farther away from whatever building you are trying to get to and walk the difference. Take the stairs instead of the escalator or elevator.
3. Turn on the tunes and dance around your living room.
4. Start riding your bike or walking to places that are reasonably distanced (subject to interpretation, of course).
5. Listen to a podcast or music as you go for a walk around the block (even better, get to a trail or natural setting).

protect you when it thinks you are under threat. Now, tune in to the senses that are available to you as you move through this meditation.

Consider **sight**. Look around and notice three things that are beautiful or interesting in your immediate environment. See if you can feel appreciation for your ability to take in those elements.

Turn your attention to **hearing**. What are three sounds you can hear right now, pleasant or unpleasant? Consider a beautiful sound you've heard recently. It might be your favorite song, the wind in the trees, or a baby laughing. How lovely to be able to savor that.

How about our sense of **touch**? In this moment, what's something

6. Start adding movement while you are watching TV or YouTube videos. Walk in place (or on a treadmill or elliptical, if you have one). Do some stretching.

7. Every day, do push-ups, sit-ups, and squats. Start with a number of repetitions that is reasonable for you (that might be just one, in the beginning), and increase that number as you get stronger. Strength builds surprisingly fast!

8. Want to try adding weights, but don't have any? Soup cans or gallon milk or detergent jugs can be substituted for traditional weights.

9. Chair yoga is a gentle way of easing into movement that isn't too demanding. Plenty of great video options are available online.

10. Wii Fit, *Dance Dance Revolution*, or any number of other gamified fitness activities can build in movement while having fun.

It's always a good idea to check in with your doctor if you are going to start building new physical habits into your routine. They can help you make the best choices for your body.

you can feel with your body? Maybe it's this book with your hands. And consider some of your favorite physical sensations: feeling the sun on your back, the softness of your puppy, or the striking of your feet against the pavement as you run hard.

Notice your **sense of smell**. What scent are you grateful for? Maybe there's a whiff of something right now that brings you joy. Maybe you recall the smell of cookies baking, eucalyptus wafting through the trees, or the scent of your best friend's house. What scents give you a feeling of ease and joy?

What about being able to **taste**? Think about a time your favorite meal was in front of you. What did that first bite taste like? How lucky to be able to take in delicious food.

And finally, think about a time you moved your body that felt so right. Maybe it was dancing alone in your house, the burning in your legs as you crossed the finish line in a cross-country meet, or simply a gentle sway side to side while listening to your favorite song. Whatever its limitations, how incredible that the body has the capacity to take in the world around us and move and shift. Can we find deep appreciation for that? Can we show care by investing in our bodies through intentional movement (balanced with intentional rest)?

How Tech Can Help

Some fitness experts suggest tracking your daily steps to assess your activity level. From the health app on your phone to fitness trackers like the Fitbit, tech provides many ways to calculate how many steps you walk a day. While many people claim ten thousand is the magical goal number, the most useful thing we can do with these calculations is to notice where we are and gradually try to beat our best. Or choose a number that is more than what you're currently doing and see how you can add steps to your routine.

Lots of free or low-cost apps also offer workout suggestions. (Of course, beware of the attention economy. We know we are giving up our attention and potentially our data in exchange for these inexpensive services.) If you are comfortable with the conditions, you can download apps with yoga videos, strength training, running training programs, and more. You can also find online fitness communities of folks who are motivating one another. (Again, be aware of what you are getting yourself into here. Are the messages affirming and supportive, or are they all about weight loss and superficial concerns? If it's the second, it's not going to be a healthy group.)

Finally, some influencers use their platforms to promote self-acceptance and care. Folks such as Megan Jayne Crabbe, Jessamyn Stanley, Kali Kushner, Troy Solomon, or Daniel Franzese are advocating for healthy body image, at every size. Aubrey Gordon and Sophia Carter-Kahn host podcasts *Maintenance Phase* and *She's All Fat*, respectively, and they are both deeply involved in fat activism. Remember, we are trying to take care of our bodies because we love them and want to enjoy them, not because we hate them and want to make them "better" in some way. Simultaneously, we can learn how to notice our own prejudices and biases and address them so that we don't participate in fat shaming and help create a healthier culture for all.

Fun Time!

While we were really good at having fun when we were kids, it can become harder to find time for fun and play as we get older. We can respond to some of the weight of increased responsibilities and seriousness that naturally become part of our lives by inviting in more playfulness and levity on purpose. If you feel self-conscious about this, an accomplice can help: Kids and pets are awesome for helping us let loose. (Maybe ask a sibling, niece or nephew, or a neighbor to join you for the activities below.)

So what might play look like? Bounce on a trampoline! Go sledding. Crank the music and dance or sing like a wild person. Construct a giant lawn waterslide in the backyard. Paint your face. Get dressed up in a Halloween costume . . . in May. Tell terrible jokes to anyone who will listen. Think about what was fun when you were five and see what happens when you give it a go.

Mindful Practice to Try

Improv games are a great way to get into the moment and challenge us to let go of our self-consciousness. Here are two simple ones to try with a group:

Human machine. One person gets into the middle of the group and starts a repeating action, such as pretending to shovel. Then the next person jumps in, pretending to catch the snow and swiveling around to dump it. A third may lie on the ground under the snow dump and logroll back and forth. Everyone joins in and the pieces of the machine work together.

Human orchestra. One person starts by making a repeating sound. They might say, "Boop, boop, boop, boop . . ." Then another person spontaneously adds, "Da . . . dada . . . da . . . dada." A third may try drumming in time on their chest. Eventually, a whole bunch of sounds create an "orchestra" together.

How Tech Can Help

Doing fun activities is a time when it might be tempting to record. But if you really want something to feel freeing, put all the phones away. Not everything we do has to be a performance! Instead, use your technology to help create the experience: to play the music or find fun group games to play together!

People Time

I don't think I need to tell you the importance of spending face-to-face time with friends and family (assuming they are supportive and loving people in your lives). The COVID-19 pandemic really highlighted how critical time with our people—people who get us, people we can be our authentic selves with—is to our well-being. It's not just about feeling good, however.

Five Fun Group Game Apps

Heads Up! A version of charades in which a player holds the phone up to their forehead and attempts to guess the word their team will describe to them. (You can also get the classic version of charades.)

Psych! Outwit Your Friends Trivia or nonsense? That's what your friends will try to guess in this trivia-based game.

Spaceteam This game involves shouting at one another as you try to fix your spaceship before it explodes.

Triple Agent! If you have a bigger group (five to nine players, so says the app), this one is for you. A small team of double agents tries to take out the official agents by making them vote to imprison their own.

Who Can't Draw Based on the classic game of telephone, one person receives a word and must draw an image to represent it. Then, one at a time, each player tries to draw the same image based on the last one, with the final player trying to guess the word.

It's important to figure out who in our lives shows us genuine care and helps us realize our best selves, and then make space for those folks. Once we are together, what can we do? I admit (with some embarrassment), when my husband and I decided to dig ourselves out of a baby-induced torpor and started spending time together again, we struggled a little to think about what we liked to do besides streaming Netflix. Sometimes it's hard to remember what's fun, and if it's been a while since we spent time with others without technology being a key part of that experience, we might need inspiration.

Tech-Free Inspiration

This list is made up of suggestions from teens and parents around what they like to do together. It is not exhaustive, so please feel free to add your own ideas!

Baking

Camping

Canoeing, kayaking, or boating

Cooking

Crafts

DIY manicure, pedicure, or face mask

Drawing

Going on a picnic

Going to the library

Having water adventures at a beach, pool, lake, or pond

Hiking

Hosting art nights (put out a bunch of supplies and pick your medium of choice: painting, drawing, sculpting, and so on)

Kicking around a ball

Listening to podcasts

Making a fire or s'mores

Playing basketball

Playing board games (Scrabble, chess, checkers, Monopoly, Sorry!, or others)

Playing catch

Playing instruments

Puzzles

Reading (or meeting with a book club)

Riding a bike

Singing

Skating at a skate park

Team games (Pictionary, charades, and so on)

Tennis

Twenty Questions

Using conversation cards (you can find tons of these online)

Visiting museums or aquariums (libraries often have free or discount passes!)

Walking

Watching a game IRL (soccer, basketball, ice hockey, and so on)

Add yours here!

Mindful Practice to Try

In the age of technology, it can be easy to ignore each other when we are together. We occupy the same physical space, but our minds are focused on our devices. We look up every now and then to share a funny TikTok video, but we don't actually spend much time physically playing basketball together or listening to one another.

The next time you are with someone, try giving your complete attention to listening to that person. Put your phone down and really take them in. As they speak, see if you can tell how they feel about what they are sharing. Are they pumped? Nervous? Annoyed?

Also, notice how *you* feel as they speak. Do you get excited with them? Jealous for something awesome they have coming up? Worried? How does your body react to what they are sharing?

Finally, notice any impulses you have. Do you want to interrupt or tell a related story? What if you just listened instead of trying to immediately share your thoughts and perspective?

See what it feels like to totally be with someone. See if they react differently to having your full attention.

If you and your friend group are not used to paying full attention to one another, at first this might feel uncomfortable or awkward. To ease that tension, you might try this practice out while you are actively doing something else, such as walking or playing a game. Remember, just because something is challenging or uncomfortable doesn't mean it's bad! We can practice paying attention to one another, and over time we'll notice what it does to our feelings of understanding and connecting to one another.

How Tech Can Help

Even if we are physically apart from our nearest and dearest, we can still gather over video platforms. Live conversations with friends and family are different and worth adding to our texting and video messaging. Even if you are communicating in this way, see if you can refrain from skipping back and forth between your conversation and other tabs or apps. What is it like to just give your whole attention to your people?

Giving Time

Sometimes, the best way we can gain perspective on our lives is to do something for someone else. When we spend energy investing in others, we get outside of our heads and experience a connection. This can be as simple as writing a note to a lonely family member or as elaborate as going on a volunteer trip to support turtle conservation in Bali. (This is an actual thing you can do. I just looked it up. As with anything, though, please do your research ahead of time to make sure you do it in a safe and ethical way!) The benefits are cascading; not only does the cared-for person (or creature) benefit, but you will also.

Caring for others can give us a larger sense of purpose. It can also have all sorts of health benefits, like making us happier, leading to lower blood pressure and even elongating our lives! The physical sensation we get when helping others is called a *helper's high*, and it's characterized by a sense of strength, vitality, calm, and compassion (for self and others). So consider adding some activities that involve giving, whether that be small random acts of kindness or something more consistent, like working at an animal shelter.

Organizations for Teen Volunteers

You could start volunteering by looking up local organizations, or you might check out these national organizations that invite teens to volunteer.

American Red Cross The American Red Cross has lots of opportunities, from helping organize a blood drive to supporting disaster relief efforts to organizing or participating in a fundraising activity.

Habitat for Humanity You can connect with your local chapter (or start a campus chapter) to participate in direct service work on homes, advocacy work for affordable housing, or fundraising to support Habitat for Humanity's work.

Animal Humane Society Animal lovers may be able to connect with a local shelter to help care for its animals or raise funds to help support such efforts.

DoSomething.org This website is a hub of volunteer campaigns specifically for young people that address a whole host of issues. You could join actions related to bullying, gun violence, racial justice, and more.

Mindful Practice to Try

It can be helpful to remember that there is a world of folks out there, all of whom all have the same basic needs and wants. We all share this common humanity. We can have compassion for people, even those we disagree with. We can wish them well. This frees up space in our hearts, if nothing else. Ever heard the old expression,

Scan to listen.

"Holding on to anger is like drinking poison and expecting the other person to die"? We can practice having kind thoughts for someone as a way of relieving our own internal pressure of holding a grudge.

It's easiest to experience a sense of connection with individuals you already care for, and then maybe you'll practice it for someone you feel tension with (like a friend who posted a dumb picture of you). This practice is not initially appropriate for someone who has caused you great harm.

Bring to mind a person you care about.

Just like me, they want to feel cared for.
Just like me, they want to feel peace.
Just like me, they want to feel at ease.

May you feel cared for.
May you feel peace.
May you feel at ease.

May we feel cared for.
May we feel peace.
May we feel at ease.

How Tech Can Help

You can find inspiration all over the internet, as well as connecting with programs that can assist you in doing volunteer work. Organizations exist to work on nearly any issue you may be passionate about, and you can often explore and become involved in these organizations online. Or you may even find a way to start your own local initiative, in which case you may need technology to communicate with others about the best way to enact your ideas.

Awe Time

Have you ever looked out from the peak of a mountain, up at a starry night sky, or even at a picture of Earth from a satellite and thought, *Whoa*? These visions can suddenly give us a sense of the vastness of our world and our smallness in it. This is such a necessary perspective. We sometimes think our problems are so huge and all-encompassing. "I'll *never* get over that jerky thing that my sibling said to me yesterday!" But if we take a moment to consider something awe-inspiring, we can invite in a perspective shift. Like, this is such a little problem in a tiny moment of my life, and I can actually be reminded of that when I connect to something bigger. That sense can help us feel less overwhelmed with smaller life struggles and put them into the context of a bigger reality. It can help us feel like we are a part of something greater than ourselves.

And we don't have to wait for awe to strike randomly. We can practice inviting in and experiencing the *Wow* to make our own lives richer.

Mindful Practice to Try

This practice can give us a sense of awe just by broadening our perspective of our physical space.

Sit or lie down comfortably. Let your eyes close or soften your gaze. Sense how your body is connected to Earth. Feel those contact points, whether at the feet or the seat. You are connected.

Scan to listen.

Gather a sense of the space around you. You are just a small body and the rest of the room is filled with objects and air. Mentally zoom out farther and notice the building you are in. If there are other people in the space, acknowledge their presence. Then acknowledge the space itself. Sense its physical structure. Imagine you are zooming out and have a sense of your building surrounded by your whole neighborhood. You might even imagine at this point that you have a bird's-eye view.

Zoom out again and consider your town or city. Keep scanning out until you have a sense of your state, your country, your continent. And there you are amid that vast space. You may even imagine going above Earth's atmosphere and looking down from a satellite's perspective, knowing the planet is teeming with people going to work, going to school, playing games, doing homework, and trying to get by.

Notice what it feels like to have this perspective.

Now slowly imagine that you are zooming back in, seeing the outline of your continent, then your country. Come in closer and notice your state from above, then your town and neighborhood.

Finally, bring your focus back into the building that you occupy, and the room, and your body.

Notice what it felt like to zoom way out and back in like that. Did it create a wave of feeling through the body? Maybe it was even a little scary at points? This is what awe can feel like in the body.

How Tech Can Help

Let's say you live in an area that isn't particularly beautiful or that doesn't naturally inspire awe, or you're stuck inside a tiny apartment amid a raging pandemic (hypothetically speaking, of course). In these cases, you can use images or songs from a device to evoke a sense of awe. Below you'll find some search terms to try. See what you can come up with. (A special thanks to Kind Mind education for the inspiration!)

Try an image search for:

- Flower bloom time-lapse
- Grand Canyon
- Parkour
- Redwoods
- Whale under boat
- (Insert your own search term for things that make you feel awe here)

You could do this same experiment with sound. Try a search for:

- Beatbox master
- One Voice Children's Choir
- Thunderstorms

While it's not going to be the same for everyone, your body will tell you when you've struck something that creates a sense of awe in you. If you do notice your body reacting with tingling, lightness, shivers, or even just shifting in any way, stay with those sensations and let yourself fully experience this moment of *Wow*.

Moving Forward

As I shared at the beginning of this book, the work to develop a healthy relationship with technology will never end. It doesn't matter how committed you were to reading this book, how much you believe in these tools and strategies, or how ardently you try to follow the suggestions. We are all human with habits and tendencies, wants and needs, stressors and impulses. We will make mistakes along the way, we will veer off our path, we will forget about our tools, or we will simply be overpowered by our habits. We won't want to practice being mindful anymore. We will want to allow ourselves to be drawn in to what is easy.

Even I find myself regularly moving toward and away from my healthiest tech life. It is not a strict set of rules for me but a dance responsive to what I notice. I delete Instagram if I find I'm too drawn in or it's not providing fulfillment, and I reinstate it if I am inspired and want to share something.

After my alarm clock died, I brought my phone into my room because I needed something to wake me up, and I found myself scrolling through TikTok until way past when my body wanted to sleep. When I recognized how bad it felt to lose precious sleep hours for a few nights in a row, I got a new alarm clock (the ones that wake you up with a natural sunrise are really nice! I highly recommend them!), found a new book to read (this is a key replacement behavior for me), and left my phone charging in the living room at night.

I get tired of writing this book and then take out my phone to look for literally anything easier than trying to come up with more words and ideas. Eventually I realize what I am doing, notice it is not in alignment with how I want to be, and get up from my desk to take a real break so that I may begin again.

The truth is, at least momentarily, it is easier not to try. It is easier not to notice. It is easier to just hop in our tech inner tube and let the tech companies' brilliant neuroscientists and psychologists whisk us away on a "happy," tech-fueled river float. It's easier to let our habits and patterns whisk us away than it is to look at those habits and ask them, *Are you getting me where I want to go? Are you creating the life I want to live?* Sometimes just asking ourselves to pause can feel Herculean. We aren't used to it. Our habits push us to stick with what we know.

Knowing this, perhaps you ask yourself, *Can I love the dance? Can I love my humanness? Can I love myself when my actions create sleep deprivation, jealousy, work backlogs, or sadness? Can I fuel my desire to keep coming back with love and care instead of shame?*

If we go into the practice of examining our tech habits by criticizing ourselves, and criticizing others, for not living up to our ideals, we won't want to keep trying. Lead with love.

In the poem "Autobiography in Five Short Chapters," Portia Nelson writes about habits as if they were a hole. First, we fall into a hole in the street, not realizing it's there. Then we notice the hole but pretend we don't, falling in again. Next, we may notice the hole and fall in again, even though we know we see it! Finally, we may choose to walk around the hole. We may even choose another street. This is a pattern you may find yourself in as you learn how to change and break habits. Of course, habits are not always as straightforward as the progression she describes. Maybe we notice we have been scrolling for over an hour one day, only to miss noticing the same behavior a week later. Maybe we choose to set a timer when we play video games one day and hop up after thirty minutes to go get some fresh air, only to hole up for a whole weekend playing games a month later. Still, we can begin again.

And still, we can value ourselves as we fall. We can value ourselves enough to try again. We can value our vision of how we'd like to be so we can begin again.

I wish you so much luck on your journey. I am excited to walk on my own path, to see what else I may discover, and to ultimately learn from you and your experiences.

May we remain open.

May we be curious.

May we delight in what we find.

May we see the opportunity to begin again.

EBM

Acknowledgments

It feels entirely insufficient to have just my name on the front of this book, for the amount of thought, care, and attention that went into it from countless people is astronomical. A giant shoutout to my husband, Micah Burger, who held it down solo on weekends with our two daughters as I squirreled myself away in my cloffice (closet-office). Thanks to my mother, Elizabeth "MiMa" Marcus, Aunties Heidi Magario and Link Klinkenberg, and Janis "Bubbe" Burger, who also spent time with my children so I had space to write. And the deepest love to Shiloh and Zoe, for continuously inspiring me to be better and do better.

Gratitude to the students of Baxter Academy for Technology and Science, King Middle School, Cape Elizabeth Middle School, and the other younger folks who let me into their world and their relationships with technology. Thank you to Doug Fagen, Taeya Boi-Doku, Ben Painter, Chelsea Ruscio, Adam Ortman, Doug Worthen, Hallie Larson, Jonathan Werner, Matthew Day, Andy Parker, and Rebecca Acabchuk for being thought partners in my process. Thank you to the countless thinkers: the writers, researchers, scientists, journalists, filmmakers, and editors who inspired my thinking around this work.

Many, many thanks to my editors, Ashley Kuehl, Shaina Olmanson, and Em Prozinski, who helped me organize my thinking and keep all my readers in mind; to Hallie Warshaw, for seeking me out and believing in my perspective; and to the people of Lerner and Zest Books for deciding to publish.

And thank you to my many teachers who have deeply impacted my learning of mindfulness along the way, and their teachers, and their teachers' teachers, for passing on their wisdom. In particular, thanks to Manny Muros, Suddha Lee, Susa Talan, Alexis Santos, Oren Jay Sofer, Megan Cowan, Chris McKenna, Vinny Ferraro, Erin Woo, and Mary Bitterrauf for your personal touches.

To anyone I may have harmed in the writing of this book, I ask for your forgiveness, and I hope you will freely share any harms with me so that I may learn and do better.

Source Notes

16 Jeremy Fagen, interview with the author, December 8, 2020.

17 Mary Kalantzis and Bill Cope, "Socrates on the Forgetfulness That Comes with Writing," New Learning Online, accessed April 24, 2021, https://newlearningonline.com/literacies/chapter-1/socrates-on-the-forgetfulness-that-comes-with-writing.

18 Chloe Corrall, interview with the author, October 25, 2019.

19 Elsie Maxwell, interview with the author, April 27, 2021.

23 "About," Black Lives Matter, retrieved April 4, 2021, https://blacklivesmatter.com/about/.

23 Victoria Rodriguez, "The Youth Activists Who Proved Critics Wrong in 2018," Mashable, December 18, 2018, https://mashable.com/article/youth-teen-activists-2018/.

24 Encyclopedia.com, 2021, https://www.encyclopedia.com/.

24 Amelia McCarley, interview with the author, April 27, 2021.

24–25 Liette Stoecklein, interview with the author, May 4, 2021.

26 Brooke Gladstone, "Breaking News Consumer's Handbook: Fake News Edition: On the Media," WNYC Studios, New York Public Radio, November 18, 2016, https://www.wnycstudios.org/podcasts/otm/segments/breaking-news-consumer-handbook-fake-news-edition.

26 K. McSpadden, "Science: You Now Have a Shorter Attention Span Than a Goldfish," *Time*, May 14, 2015, https://time.com/3858309/attention-spans-goldfish/#:~:text=The average attention span,digitalized lifestyle on the brain.

28 Chris Berdik, "Has New Hampshire Found the Secret to Online Education that Works?" The Hechinger Report, August 4, 2016, https://hechingerreport.org/new-hampshire-found-secret-online-education-works/.

30 David Rock and Heidi Grant, "Why Diverse Teams Are Smarter," *Harvard Business Review*, November 4, 2016, https://hbr.org/2016/11/why-diverse-teams-are-smarter.

36–37 Hilary Anderson, "Social Media Apps Are 'Deliberately' Addictive to Users," BBC News, July 4, 2018, https://www.bbc.com/news/technology-44640959.

38 "Careers," Instagram, May 14, 2021, https://about.instagram.com/about-us/careers.

38 Jonathan Shieber, "Dopamine Labs Slings Tools to Boost and Reduce App Addiction," TechCrunch, February 13, 2017, https://techcrunch.com/2017/02/13/dopamine-labs-slings-tools-to-boost-and-reduce-app-addiction/.

40   Kendra Cherry, "How Does the Color Red Impact Your Mood and Behavior?" Verywell Mind, accessed April 17, 2021, https://www.verywellmind.com/the-color-psychology-of-red-2795821#:~:text=Red%20is%20also%20used%20to,in%20a%20non-literal%20way.&text=People%20tend%20to%20associate%20red,of%20poisonous%20or%20dangerous%20animals.

41   Ashton May, interview with the author, October 25, 2019.

42   Patricio O'Gorman, "Here's How Fortnite 'Hooked' Millions," Nir and Far, February 24, 2021, https://www.nirandfar.com/fortnite-hooked-millions/.

43   Julian Morgans, "Your Addiction to Social Media Is No Accident," *VICE*, 2017, https://www.vice.com/en/article/vv5jkb/the-secret-ways-social-media-is-built-for-addiction.

44   Marco Silva, "Flat Earth: How Did YouTube Help Spread a Conspiracy Theory?" BBC Reel, BBC, July 30, 2019, https://www.bbc.com/reel/video/p07h3yc0/flat-earth-how-did-youtube-help-spread-a-conspiracy-theory-.

46   Corral, interview, October 2019.

47   Dan Siegel, "Daniel Siegel: Why Teens Turn from Parents to Peers," YouTube, Greater Good Science Center, July 23, 2014, https://www.youtube.com/watch?v=thxlUme7Pc8.

50   Shirin Ghaffary and Alex Kantrowitz, "Don't Be Evil Isn't a Normal Company Value. But Google Isn't a Normal Company," Vox, February 16, 2021, https://www.vox.com/recode/2021/2/16/22280502/google-dont-be-evil-land-of-the-giants-podcast.

53   Shane Barker, "How Social Media Is Influencing Purchase Decisions," Social Media Week, May 26, 2017, https://socialmediaweek.org/blog/2017/05/social-media-influencing-purchase-decisions/.

53   Madeline Berg, "The Highest-Paid YouTube Stars Of 2020," *Forbes*, Forbes Magazine, April 13, 2021, https://www.forbes.com/sites/maddieberg/2020/12/18/the-highest-paid-youtube-stars-of-2020/?sh=65738f5f6e50.

55   "Technology's Impact on Health: Anxiety, Depression, and Social Network Use," Dignity Health, accessed April 18, 2021, https://www.dignityhealth.org/articles/technologys-impact-on-health-anxiety-depression-and-social-network-use.

55   Fran Molloy and Mark Williams, "Smartphones Are Making Us Stupid—and May Be a 'Gateway Drug'," The Lighthouse (Macquarie University, January 10, 2020), https://lighthouse.mq.edu.au/article/august-2019/smartphones-are-making-us-stupid-and-may-be-a-gateway-drug.

55 Ansuya Harjani, "Mobile Addiction Growing at an Alarming Rate," CNBC, April 24, 2014. https://www.cnbc.com/2014/04/24/mobile -addiction-growing-at-an-alarming-rate.html.

56 Tracy Dennis-Tiwary, "Can't Fight This Feeling: Technology and Teen Anxiety." *Psychology Today*, Sussex Publishers, December 11, 2017. https://www.psychologytoday.com/us/blog/more-feeling/201712 /can-t-fight-feeling-technology-and-teen-anxiety.

56 Lulu Garcia-Navarro, "The Risk of Teen Depression and Suicide Is Linked to Smartphone Use, Study Says," NPR, December 17, 2017, https://www.npr.org/2017/12/17/571443683/the-call-in-teens-and -depression.

56 Donna Vickroy, "Technology Triggers Teen Depression," *The Star Online*, November 29, 2019, https://www.thestar.com.my/tech/tech -news/2018/01/08/technology-triggers-teen-depression.

57 C.L. Odgers and M. R. Jensen, (2020), Annual Research Review: Adolescent mental health in the digital age: facts, fears, and future directions. J Child Psychol Psychiatry, 61: 336-348. https://doi.org /10.1111/jcpp.13190.

57 "Technology Use Explains at Most 0.4% of Adolescent Wellbeing," University of Oxford, January 15, 2019, https://www.ox.ac.uk/news /2019-01-15-technology-use-explains-most-04-adolescent-wellbeing.

60 Victoria L. Dunckley, *Reset Your Child's Brain: A Four-Week Plan to End Meltdowns, Raise Grades, and Boost Social Skills by Reversing the Effects of Electronic Screen-Time.* (Novato, CA: New World Library, 2015).

62 David Railton, "Just 1 Hour of Gaming May Improve Attention," Medical News Today (MediLexicon International, 2018), https://www .medicalnewstoday.com/articles/320943.

63 Tzipi Horowitz-Kraus and John S. Hutton, "Brain Connectivity in Children Is Increased by the Time They Spend Reading Books and Decreased by the Length of Exposure to Screen-Based Media." *Acta Paediatrica* 107, no. 4 (December 7, 2017): 685–93. https://doi.org /https://doi.org/10.1111/apa.14176.

63 Nicholas Carr, *The Shallows: What the Internet Is Doing to Our Brains* (New York: W. W. Norton & Co., 2011).

64 Jill Barshay, "Evidence Increases for Reading on Paper Instead of Screens," *The Hechinger Report*, April 8, 2021, https://hechingerreport .org/evidence-increases-for-reading-on-paper-instead-of-screens.

64 Mark Nichols, "Reading and Studying on the Screen: An Overview of Literature Towards Good Learning Design Practice," Journal of Open, Flexible, Distance Learning 20, no. 1, 2016, https://files.eric.ed.gov /fulltext/EJ1112348.pdf.

66 Anne Chemin, "Handwriting vs Typing: Is the Pen Still Mightier than the Keyboard?" *The Guardian*, Guardian News and Media, December 16, 2014, https://www.theguardian.com/science/2014/dec/16 /cognitive-benefits-handwriting-decline-typing.

66 Daniel M. Oppenheimer and Pam A Mueller, "The Pen Is Mightier Than the Keyboard: Advantages of Longhand Over Laptop Note Taking," SAGE Journals, Association for Psychological Science, 2014. https://journals.sagepub.com/doi/abs/10.1177/0956797614524581.

68–69 epipheo, *"What the Internet Is Doing to Our Brains,"* YouTube, 2013, https://www.youtube.com/watch?v=cKaWJ72x1rI.

69 Laurel J. Felt and Michael B. Robb, "Technology Addiction: Concern, Controversy, and Finding Balance," A Common Sense Media Brief, Common Sense Media, 2016, https://www.commonsensemedia.org /sites/default/files/uploads/research/csm_2016_technology_addiction_ research_brief_1.pdf.

69 Michael Robb, "Screens and Sleep. The New Normal: Teens, Screens, and Sleep in the United States," Common Sense Media, 2019, https:// www.commonsensemedia.org/sites/default/files/uploads/research/2019 -new-normal-parents-teens-screens-and-sleep-united-states-report.pdf.

70–71 Parekh, Ranna, ed, "Internet Gaming," American Psychiatric Association, June 2018, https://www.psychiatry.org/patients-families/internet-gaming.

71 "Mental Health and Behavioral Addiction Treatment: ReSTART®," reSTART Internet Video Game Addiction Treatment, VR Addiction, May 9, 2019, https://www.netaddictionrecovery.com/what-we-treat/.

71 "Addictive Behaviours: Gaming Disorder," World Health Organization, 2018, https://www.who.int/news-room/q-a-detail/addictive-behaviours -gaming-disorder.

72 Robb, "Screens and Sleep."

72 Tara Haelle, "Use of Electronic Devices May Reduce Sleep Among Teenagers," *Neurology Reviews* 23, no. 3 (March 2015): 26–26. https:// www.mdedge.com/neurology/article/97560/sleep-medicine/use -electronic-devices-may-reduce-sleep-among-teenagers.

73 Daniel J. Siegel, *Brainstorm: The Power and Purpose of the Teenage Brain* (New York: Jeremy P. Tarcher/Penguin, 2013).

74 Ruthann Richter, "Among Teens, Sleep Deprivation an Epidemic," Stanford Medicine, October 8, 2015, https://med.stanford.edu/news /all-news/2015/10/among-teens-sleep-deprivation-an-epidemic .html#:~:text=Sleep%20deprivation%20increases%20the%20 likelihood,suicide%20and%20even%20suicide%20attempts.

76   "Computer Vision Syndrome (Digital Eye Strain)," American Optometric Association, accessed April 20, 2021, https://www.aoa.org/healthy-eyes/eye-and-vision-conditions/computer-vision-syndrome?sso=y.

76   David DeWitt, "Text Neck Symptoms and Diagnosis," Spine-Health: Knowledge from Veritas, Veritas Health, October 26, 2018, https://www.spine-health.com/conditions/neck-pain/text-neck-symptoms-and-diagnosis.

76   M. S. Tremblay, A. G. LeBlanc, M. E. Kho et al, "Systematic review of sedentary behaviour and health indicators in school-aged children and youth," *Int J Behav Nutr Phys Act 8*, 98 (2011). https://doi.org/10.1186/1479-5868-8-98.

76   "Making Physical Activity a Way of Life: AAP Policy Explained," HealthyChildren.org, American Academy of Pediatrics, May 8, 2020, https://www.healthychildren.org/English/healthy-living/fitness/Pages/Making-Fitness-a-Way-of-Life.aspx.

78   Richard Harris, "Got Water? Most Kids, Teens Don't Drink Enough," NPR, June 11, 2015, https://www.npr.org/sections/health-shots/2015/06/11/413674246/got-water-most-kids-teens-dont-drink-enough#:~:text=The%20Institute%20of%20Medicine%20says,than%20girls%20do%2C%20research%20suggests.

82   Randy J. Semple, Vita Droutman, and Brittany Anne Reid, "Mindfulness Goes to School: Things Learned (So Far) from Research and Real-World Experiences." 2019. Psychology in the schools, 54(1), 29–52. https://doi.org/10.1002/pits.21981.

83   John LaRosa, "$1.2 Billion U.S. Meditation Market Growing Strongly as It Becomes More Mainstream," *Market Research Blog*, October 16, 2019, https://blog.marketresearch.com/1.2-billion-u.s.-meditation-market-growing-strongly-as-it-becomes-more-mainstream.

85   Oprah Winfrey, "What Oprah Knows about the Power of Meditation," Oprah.com, June 15, 2016, https://www.oprah.com/inspiration/what-oprah-knows-about-the-power-of-meditation.

87   iBme, "FAQS for Youth," accessed May 5, 2021, https://ibme.com/faq/youth/.

91   "Together, we can align technology with humanity's best interests." Center for Humane Technology, accessed April 21, 2021, https://www.humanetech.com/rebuild.

95   David Rock, Daniel J. Siegel, Steven A.Y. Poelmans, and Jessica Payne, "The Healthy Mind Platter," *NeuroLeadership Journal*, no. 4 (October 2012), https://davidrock.net/files/02_The_Healthy_Mind_Platter_US.pdf.

104 "Habit," Merriam-Webster, accessed April 22, 2021, https://www.merriam-webster.com/dictionary/habit.

106 Manuel Gámez-Guadix and Esther Calvete, "Assessing the Relationship between Mindful Awareness and Problematic Internet Use among Adolescents," *Mindfulness* 7, no. 4 (June 29, 2016), https://doi.org/10.1007/s12671-016-0566-0.

107 Ari Terry, "Q&A with a Gaming Addict in Recovery," TAG Counseling, June 25, 2018, https://tagcounseling.com/qa-with-a-gaming-addict-in-recovery/.

114 "Study shows smartphones harm the environment," Faculty of Engineering, McMaster University, February 28, 2018, https://www.eng.mcmaster.ca/news/study-shows-smartphones-harm-environment.

115 Insung Lee, "You Did It! Samsung Chooses Renewable Energy!" Greenpeace International, June 14, 2018, accessed July 2, 2021, https://www.greenpeace.org/international/story/17140/you-did-it-samsung-chooses-renewable-energy/.

117 Meeri Kim, "Blue Light from Electronics Disturbs Sleep, Especially for Teenagers," *The Washington Post*, WP Company, September 1, 2014, https://www.washingtonpost.com/national/health-science/blue-light-from-electronics-disturbs-sleep-especially-for-teenagers/2014/08/29/3edd2726-27a7-11e4-958c-268a320a60ce_story.html.

124 Clive Thompson, "How Being Bored Out of Your Mind Makes You More Creative," *Wired*, Conde Nast, September 11, 2018, https://www.wired.com/2017/01/clive-thompson-7/.

125 Elsie Maxwell, interview with the author, April 27, 2021.

130 Jill Suttie, "How Smartphones Are Killing Conversation," Greater Good Science Center, University of California, Berkeley, December 7, 2015, https://greatergood.berkeley.edu/article/item/how_smartphones_are_killing_conversation.

135 Molly McKibben, interview with the author, May 4, 2021.

138 Jean M. Twenge, Brian H. Spitzberg, and W. Keith Campbell, "Less In-Person Social Interaction with Peers among U.S. Adolescents in the 21st Century and Links to Loneliness," *Journal of Social and Personal Relationships 36*, no. 6 (June 2019): 1892–1913. https://doi.org/10.1177/0265407519836170.

138 Katherine Hobson, "Feeling Lonely? Too Much Time on Social Media May Be Why," NPR, March 6, 2017, https://www.npr.org/sections/health-shots/2017/03/06/518362255/feeling-lonely-too-much-time-on-social-media-may-be-why.

140 Oren Jay Sofer and Joseph Goldstein, *Say What You Mean: A Mindful Approach to Nonviolent Communication*. Boulder, CO: Shambhala Publications, Inc, 2018.

140   Rachel Ehmke, "What Selfies Are Doing to Girls' Self-Esteem," Child Mind Institute, June 3, 2019, https://childmind.org/article/what-selfies-are-doing-to-girls-self-esteem/.

140–141   Madelyn Peppard, interview with the author, April 27, 2021.

141   Elena Rosenberg, interview with the author, May 4, 2021.

141   Elle Hunt, "Faking It: How Selfie Dysmorphia Is Driving People to Seek Surgery," *The Guardian*, Guardian News and Media, January 23, 2019, https://www.theguardian.com/lifeandstyle/2019/jan/23/faking-it-how-selfie-dysmorphia-is-driving-people-to-seek-surgery#:~:text=The%20phenomenon%20of%20people%20requesting,clinics%20in%20London%20and%20Newcastle.

145–146   Daniyal Malik, "Research Proves 'Influencer' As One of the Most Popular Career Options Among Children," Digital Information World, February 3, 2019, https://www.digitalinformationworld.com/2019/02/young-affiliates-children-aspire-to-be-social-media-influencers-youtubers.html.

156   Julia Cameron, *The Artist's Way: A Spiritual Path to Higher Creativity* (New York: J.P. Tarcher/Putnam, 2020).

158   Markham Heid, "The Science Behind Eureka Moments," Medium, Elemental, August 28, 2019, https://elemental.medium.com/the-science-behind-eureka-moments-6729e3ce4de7.

162   Michael Pollan, *In Defense of Food: An Eater's Manifesto* (New York: Penguin Books, 2008).

167   "The Scientific Power of Thought," ASAP Science, YouTube, 2013, https://www.youtube.com/watch?v=-v-IMSKOtoE&list=PLvFsG9gYFxY907xODmFk-faD6uO0a3gMh&index=32.

168   Amy Saltzman, *A Still Quiet Place for Athletes: Mindfulness Skills for Achieving Peak Performance and Finding Flow in Sports and Life* (Oakland, CA: New Harbinger Publications, 2018).

178   Christine Carter, "What We Get When We Give," Greater Good Science Center, University of California, Berkeley, February 18, 2010, https://greatergood.berkeley.edu/article/item/what_we_get_when_we_give.

179   "Be a Volunteer," American Red Cross Youth, American Red Cross, June 19, 2020, http://redcrossyouth.org/scholarships/be-a-volunteer/.

179   "Youth Programs," Habitat for Humanity, Habitat for Humanity International, https://www.habitat.org/volunteer/near-you/youth-programs.

179   "Join Our Youth-Led Movement for Good," DoSomething.org, https://join.dosomething.org/.

185   Portia Nelson, "Autobiography in Five Short Chapters," Mindfulness Association, 2020, https://www.mindfulnessassociation.net/words-of-wonder/autobiography-in-five-short-chapters-portia-nelson/.

Recommended Resources

Bocci, Goali Saidi. *The Social Media Workbook for Teens*. Oakland, CA: Instant Help Books, 2019.

Brewer, Judson. *The Craving Mind: From Cigarettes to Smartphones to Love— Why We Get Hooked and How We Can Break Bad Habits*. New Haven, CT: Yale University Press, 2017.

Carr, Nicholas. *The Shallows: What the Internet Is Doing to Our Brains*. New York: W.W. Norton & Co., 2011.

Center for Humane Technology
https://www.humanetech.com/

Common Sense Media
commonsensemedia.com

Crouch, Amy, and Andy Crouch: *My Tech-Wise Life: Growing Up and Making Choices in a World of Devices*. Grand Rapids, MI: Baker Books, 2020.

Price, Catherine: *How to Break Up with Your Phone*. New York: Ten Speed Press, 2018.

Screenagers: Growing Up in the Digital Age. Film. Produced and directed by Delaney Rushton. Seattle: MyDoc Productions, 2016.

Siegel, Daniel J. *Brainstorm: The Power and Purpose of the Teenage Brain*. New York: Tarcher/Penguin, 2013.

The Social Dilemma. Netflix film. Produced by Larissa Rhodes, directed by Jeff Orlowski. Boulder, CO: Exposure Labs, 2020.

Index

About the Author

Erica Marcus continues to strive for balance in her own tech life (and life in general) from her home in Portland, Maine, where she lives with her two small kiddos and husband. For almost two decades, she has had the privilege of working alongside and learning from young people in various capacities: from a wilderness youth therapy setting in Utah to teaching English at a Washington, DC, charter school to offering mindfulness in various schools in Maine. As a recovering perfectionist with a fierce inner critic, she has slowly developed her understanding of awareness and compassion practices through yoga and meditation traditions, including Kripalu yoga, Anusara yoga, Insight Meditation, mindfulness-based stress reduction, and other lineages. She is a certified Mindful Schools instructor, Kripalu yoga teacher, and WholeSchool Mindfulness director for an area middle school. She likes to balance her tech use with hiking, trail running, surfing, reading fiction, hanging out with friends and family, and eating ice cream.